Father's
last
Joke.

by

Pat.

Chapter One.

It was in March 1902 when Martha was born in Derby, Connecticut, midst a heavy snow storm at three o'clock in the morning. My father had to dig his way out to bring the doctor. I was their eighth child and I feel sure I was my father's last joke. He promised my mother there would be no more children. They could barely afford this eighth child. My eldest sister who helped to bring up all these children, would be upset if mother didn't come down for breakfast. She knew that there would be another baby to care for, and mother promised her that there would be no more babies after the eighth one. Two had been still born, or had died very young, I don't know; but six was still a handful for her.

I was a very sick baby for the first year. I nearly died. It seems I had to live for some reason, for a very interesting life that followed.

In those days doctors would take the birth registrations and the name of the child. He was told my name was Martha Sophia Dean and I was later christened as such. Five years later when we moved back to England where my parents came from, we sent for my birth papers, and I had been registered as Estelle Dean. We returned the papers to say they were wrong as my name should be Martha Sophia. They sent them back again to say that my name had been registered as Estelle Dean and that must be my official name. Well, we came to the conclusion that the doctor must have had two births that morning and got the names mixed up.

I wonder where Martha Sophia is. I hope she likes her name. Or maybe my doctor was sorry for me and changed my name to Estelle. Whoever you were at the time of my birth, I thank you for changing my name. My sisters decided to call me Pat, so I've been Pat all my life.

When I became five years of age my mother gave me a birthday party for all the children who lived nearby. Two weeks after, two of the sisters who came to my party died of some kind of fever. This was a shock to all. It caused my mother to have a nervous breakdown. My father suggested she should take a trip back to England to see her mother, and take the six surviving children. It was to be for six weeks. But mother didn't want to return to the USA again, so father had to sell all their belongings except the sewing machine and the piano. He brought them over because he knew mom wanted to sew our clothes and my older sister was learning to play the piano.

I remember the day we docked in Liverpool, it was raining very hard. We took the train to a little Lancashire town called Accrington. When we got to the station, all seven of us packed into a cab, and arrived at Grandma's house. It was only a three bedroom and one bathroom to house twelve people. It was still raining and we children started to cry, we all hated it.

Grandma and Grandpa were about sixty years old. Grandpa went to work at five o'clock every morning and worked until five at night. In the mornings he was a knocker-up. He had a long pole with wire strings on the end and he would hit people's bedroom windows with it until they answered, "All right." I guess he parted more couples than the local courts and Judges did. In the evenings he was a lamplighter. He must have walked miles every night to light the street gas lamps. Grandpa must have been a healthy man, he lived till he was nearly ninety. He was a likeable fellow.

We moved into our own house when father came over. He got a job in a factory. The older girls went into a weaving factory, but didn't like it. As I grew up I wasn't going to be put into a weaving factory. I left school at the age of twelve. For two years I did half a day at school and half a day at a workroom to learn dressmaking. After that I remember my sister and I had to walk two miles to work at the workroom, and worked from 8:30 am until eight o'clock at night six days a week. Saturday was a half day's work. We used to work two nights a week overtime until ten o'clock, I was fourteen years old at the time. We had to be sixteen before we were allowed to work all those hours. One night I was working and about nine o'clock the factory inspector came to have a look round. I was pushed into a cupboard out of sight till he was gone. I remember my pay was so little they paid me every two weeks.

The First World War was on. I was going to work one morning and there was a battalion of soldiers marching past me. Their wives were running alongside them crying. These men were on their way to France to fight in the trenches and would not come home for many months. I so well remember the military band playing 'It's a long way to Tipperary'. I was too young to realise this unhappy scene and the anguish these wives were going through. This may be the last time they would see each other.

There was this story about two soldiers. They were in the trenches in France, they had been there nearly two years. One of them got a letter from his wife to say she had just given birth to a beautiful baby boy. He told his friend in the excitement, "Hey Bill, I am a father. The wife's just had a baby. Isn't that wonderful?" His pal replied, "That can't be true. You haven't been home for two years." Joe replied, "Oh, that's all right Bill, You know there's two years between me and my brother." (Could be?) .

I worked at dressmaking until I was fifteen when my older sister and I opened a dressmaking and tailoring shop. I made myself my first costume at the age of fifteen. I was sure proud to wear it. At the time the hobble skirt was in fashion. One had to be very careful how one walked.

My father and brother worked in London on munitions. They earned good money till the end of the war. My older brother was in the army. He died of a war wound.

The war was over and my sisters got married, as well as my only brother. I was the only one at home. My parents bought a very nice hotel. I helped in the bar and had many men admirers. I was now eighteen years of age and had grown a very attractive personality with good looks. I was a well sought after person. I had lots of wealthy men friends. I became a self centred person, I thought I had the world on a string. These men really spoiled me. Some were married and some were eligible bachelors such as doctors, lawyers, mill owners, all who had a lot to offer me in marriage.

One man was the son of a Sir, a very wealthy family. He really did make me some very tempting offers. He was the first person to teach me to drive a car. His car, a big Chrysler. He was much older than I, but my father knew him as a brother Freemason and seemed a very honourable man. One evening he came in with a gift for my twentieth birthday. I didn't open it until he had left the pub. I was shocked to see it was a beautiful diamond ring with a note attached, 'Darling I love you. Please accept this as a token of my love.' Well, I guessed that if I did accept this ring I would be under an obligation to him, so I decided to return it to him when he came into the pub again. He didn't like that at all. I realised later that he thought he had bought me body and soul.

I tried to cool him away from me. I could see he was not the marrying type and besides, he was too old for me. All he wanted was a mistress. He promised me a house at the beach, a car, a maid to do all the housework for me. That life didn't appeal to me. I wanted a husband. I found out later he had a wife and a daughter as old as I. I was so glad I had the guts to hold no to my 'virginity'. That was the end of that romance.

In this pub business barmaids meet many men with many offers. One fellow took photographs of me for a well known magazine. He also got me film tests. I guess I could have gone into films, but what would that have cost me? No, that didn't appeal to me. I got several invitations for a gay weekend in Paris, but I knew good girls never went to Paris. You paid for all you got, bodily. That didn't interest me. This pub life was very fascinating and I was loving the glamour.

I had met several prostitutes. They would tell me of their experiences that were shocking. They were a kindly type of girl. They would cross the street to give a beggar a pound note they had just earned a few minutes before. I found these girls had hearts of gold. They would help anyone who needed it, and would give their bodies on a promise.

We had homosexuals too. In those days you could tell who they were by their make up, lipstick etc. Here again these men were kind and generous. I always felt sorry for them. I was a good listener to all their troubles. When they got too much to drink they would talk about their mothers. With tears in their eyes they would say, "I have broken my mother's heart", and they were very sorry for it. I tried to help them, but they told me once you become a homo you never change as long as you live. They would sometimes get beaten up by fellows who hated them. I always had a soft spot for this kind of person. Who are we to judge? These are some of the characters you meet in the hotel business. It is an education. I shall always love it.

We lived in this pub for six years. My parents bought another one in the heart of Manchester amongst all the business warehouses and offices. This was a very busy pub. Lots of wealthy Jews in the cotton trade were our customers. We got the same class of people who to me, were very interesting. I liked to listen to their troubles and tried to help them.

I had many offers if marriage, but I was having too many flirtations. I wasn't ready to settle down. My father got quite concerned about this and told me a story about Mary. Her father asked her to walk up their garden path and bring back the prettiest flower in the garden, without turning back. Mary kept on walking up the path, passing some beautiful flowers. She thought there must be prettier flowers higher up the path. She came back to her father with a weed. "Now Mary, that's not a flower."

"But daddy, I was hoping to find a more beautiful flower higher up the garden."

So my father told me, "Let that be a warning to you, Don't pass up good offers of marriage, or you will come up with a weed, a no good." At that time I was very confused about marrying anyone. I was having a wonderful time with many of the customers. I didn't seem to have any problems. Marriage was out for me just then.

We landlords use to visit other pubs in the area. I used to visit a pub just down the street where a young couple managed. They had an eight year old daughter who was learning ballet. One day when I was there this little girl danced for us. We all clapped and told her, "One day, Margot, you will be famous." Yes, she did become famous. She is Dame Margot Fontaine, the tops in ballet. A beautiful lady I have alway admired and who has given me encouragement in thoughts of self achievement.

I had many dreams that didn't come true. I felt I always wanted to make people laugh. I had a terrific sense of humour that stayed with me all my life when I was under great stress.

My father died suddenly, that was a great loss to me. We knew each other's thought world and had a great understanding between us. Then, a year later, my mother passed on. That left me with the responsibility of the pub.

Chapter Two.

Just before mom died I had met who I thought was Mr. Right. He was a charmer, a good business man. I married him within three months. I sold the pub and we lived in a nice apartment. His job took him abroad often. He was in the cotton trade. Within the first six months of our marriage I realised I had married an alcoholic. I was in a state of shock. I couldn't believe I could make this kind of mistake in marriage. After my father's warning I thought I was smart. My husband was away much of the time so I didn't recognise his drinking until he lost his job in 1931.

That was the big slump in the cotton industry in England. These were terrible years for people all over the world. I had to start to do sewing. I worked up a good business that kept the wolf from our door for a while. He was a black coat worker. He couldn't draw any unemployment money, so I had to earn it. There was no work for him; he did get some small jobs, but they didn't last long on account of his drinking. He would spend all his earnings on drink. I was in a desperate state of mind, now that I discovered I pregnant. How could I bring a child into this state I was in? My world had fallen apart. I was hating myself for accepting this situation now, but I had to take it.

We had a son. Maybe he would be a godsend for me. We christened him Fred. He became a blessing for me as the years went by. We moved to a ten roomed house so we could let out some of the rooms to help pay the rent. We had many years of struggling to pay the rent man, the milk man.

We were owing the rent man. He would knock hard on the front door and I wouldn't answer. He would shout so the neighbours could hear him, "Rent over due." Then he brought Bill Bailey, (the bailiffs). If they get into your house they could take away all your belongings and strip the house for the rent that was owed. They could also put you out of your house. We would have nowhere to sleep, so I kept my doors locked. We sure had some fun and games with that rent collector. He would go to the back door and try to get through the window. This, a drunken man, and sewing, really got me down.

And I thought I'd married Mr. Right. The only time I saw him was after the pubs were closed at ten o'clock. Then I had to wait till he got to sleep before we could go to our beds. He would fall asleep anywhere, in a chair or on the floor. I didn't know an alcoholic suffered from hallucinations. He said he had all kinds of things chasing him. He would shout at me to chase them away. My nerves were so bad the doctor put me on a strong drug. I was worried about my little boy too. It was unfair that he should see all this. One day I was busy sewing and the spool on the sewing machine would suddenly come empty, which did annoy me. My little boy came and put his arm round me and said, "Mommy when I am a big boy I will make a spool that will never come empty." What a thought, bless him. And I was still doing sewing, I made all my own clothes and his jackets.

I had years of this trouble. One day I collapsed and was taken to hospital. I had severe haemorrhaging, I nearly died. My son was taken to the hospital with pneumonia. I had to have a hysterectomy. I was pleased about that, I didn't want any more children, but I would have loved a daughter. I was in the hospital six weeks. They brought my little boy to be with me in the same hospital, I knew he was safe with me. This hospital was for poor people, it was known as the 'Work House'. I met some queer people in there. The woman in the next bed was a prostitute. She told me she came in for an abortion three times a year, her husband was a sailor. The nurses knew her. She told me some funny stories of the men she had met. The trouble was, she was a foul mouthed person, and I was feeling pretty fed up. She told me what the hospital was giving us for dinner that day. "Listen love, we are having spotted dick for dessert." Said with a big wink and a crude laugh. What a woman! I was glad when she left.

I was crying one day and the lady across from me came over and talked to me. She was so kind. I told her my troubles, she was a good listener and helped me a great deal. I guess I felt sorry for myself until she told me her troubles. It made mine look small. Her husband was in jail for five years for incest. Their daughter had a baby by him. She had two daughters, he was very strict and seemed a devoted father. He never allowed them to have friends, he would go for walks with them and buy them gifts. At the age of twenty five one had the baby. She told me she has not looking forward to his homecoming in five years time. After all that I thought I wasn't too badly off. There is always someone worse off than you, if you knew of it, so I guess I must count my blessings and pray for others.

When I came out of hospital I went to see a Catholic priest to tell him my problems. He advised me to let my son go into a Catholic convent away from that environment. He would become a Catholic, and that I didn't like. I told him I would let him know later. I considered this very seriously and decided not to let him go to the convent, as the Second World War was about to start. I felt I couldn't part with him. He was part of me. Everything was very unsettled now. There was an air of excitement that the war would start any day. Hitler wanted it.

We had rented four bed sitting rooms to men who were unemployed. That helped to pay our rent every week. Joe, one of these men, was very helpful to me. He had been badly shot up in the first World War and couldn't work. But he sure helped me move furniture around the house. Joe was a blessing to me. He would come down some mornings to my kitchen and sit and have a cuppa with me, tea or coffee, and try to cheer me up with his funny stories. Joe would tell me of the most fantastic experiences he had in his past life. He said when he was about fourteen he used to visit an old lady who had trouble sleeping. He would go to her house. He didn't say how old she was, but to him at fourteen she was an old lady who needed help to make her sleep. Joe would tickle the bottoms of her feet until she laughed herself to sleep. She paid him tuppence an hour (two pence). That was quite good pay in those days. I asked him why he did that, he replied the money was good. She must have experienced a strange pleasure form Joe's tickling. Maybe this could have been the start of these massage parlours. Joe could have made a fortune had he continued the tickling of all parts of the body. Who knows?

One morning Joe told me the tallest story I have ever heard. He said it was a true story. On his travels abroad he met an eastern fellow. He said they got talking about sex, how, and which way one could have an exotic reaction. He told Joe the man would tie a cord to his manhood and tie the other end to his big toe. When the fun started he would wriggle his big toe. That would shake his manhood and give the ladies a great thrill. I had never heard of such a thing. I guess it could be done, but you might strangle your best friend or finish up with gout in your big toe. I guess you can't have everything.

Joe was a tonic for me. Many times he would help me bail out my husband from jail for drunk driving. Joe said he had worked on a farm miles away from the next one. When he was quite young he worked in the potato fields. He used to cut a hole in a potato and stick a little note inside hoping that someone would find it. Perhaps a kitchen maid in one of the big houses or castles would find it. This is how he met his wife. He told me he got many replies from the potato love notes.

Joe was a great help to me. He had many opportunities to proposition me, but he never did. He was always a gentleman, and a good listener. I really had to rely on him for help. I had many dreams of a real man, but it wasn't Joe. After three years he left to live with his lady friend. I missed Joe in many ways. He was always there when I needed him.

My husband would bring home different men he had met during the time he was working. One evening he brought home the wrong man. He was a tall good looking man. When he shook my hand, I knew he was the man I had dreamed of to marry. He had appeared unexpectedly. It seemed he would be around us often. He made excuses to see me, and every time I saw him I could feel a stronger attraction between us. I tried not to accept this situation, but we found we were two helpless people who had fallen in love at first sight. Tom had not even kissed me, How could we be in love? I was very sure of my feelings for him. This was the most unexpected love affair I could ever have wished for.

He was in his forties. It became very difficult for us not to show our feelings for each other. He became my lover, not a sexual affair, just a boy and girl love affair. He told me that his wife had been an invalid for many years. That shocked me and made me feel very guilty. We were both at the stage where we were about to give way to our sexual urges.

We both needed each other. How long could we refrain from this disturbing love affair? We talked things over, again and again, but it didn't seem fair to us that we should give up seeing each other. I didn't think I could live without seeing Tom. He had become more like a brother. Then, I didn't see him for two weeks and I couldn't understand why. My husband gave me the news, Tom had to go into hospital for a very serious operation. He had died on the operating table. What a shock it gave me! I couldn't believe I would never see Tom again. Well, I guess that's the answer to my prayers. Our love was not to be.

My husband got another job and we had to move to the north east of England. World War Two had started. We lived there for just twelve months then moved inland to Newcastle upon Tyne. The raids from Hitler got worse. We nearly lived in the shelters. We lived on the second floor apartment of a three story house. Its walls were nearly two feet thick, so we thought we were safe from the bombs. We would go to the basement when the raids started. One night Hitler dropped a land mine in the street behind our house. This well built house shook like a leaf. My little boy was with me. We sat on a stone shelf. It was a large walk-in closet, I expect where all the bottled fruit etc., had been stored. I put a large pillow on top of my little boy's head to protect him, but that would be no good if we got a direct hit. Believe me, we said our prayers that night. My husband had not come home. The raid lasted for five hours. I was very concerned about my little boy's safety. I decided he should be evacuated to a safer place.

It was long past midnight one night when the police brought my husband home. He was found fast asleep in the middle of the road, fortunately there was almost no traffic. He was lucky to be alive. Can one imagine, with all the bombs dropping and the guns firing, he could fall asleep? He must have been very drunk. I guess God looks after his own, so they tell me.

Two weeks later I took my son to a place we thought would be safe, on a farm in Cumberland. He was very happy there amongst the animals. I visited him once a month. I decided to get a job. I drove a large van for the Joe Lyons Tea Company. I had to go to London to pass my driving test. I was in London for two nights. This was during the fire of London, the worst raids of the war. We spent all our nights in the shelters.

I have never seen so many fires. Wherever you looked London was on fire. This was the biggest fire raid of the war, and I was in the middle of it. In the mornings we saw men with large sacks picking up arms etc. Their faces were black from the fires. Some had tears streaming down their faces. I wept too. I could not take this. I was so proud of those brave people in London. You had to be there to know the tragedy those bombings caused.

I didn't get to take my driving test, so they sent an inspector up to me, and I did pass my test. I loved my job, but those air raids would come more often. Driving through the days when the sirens went, I would pull up my van and run to the nearest shelter, hoping my van would be there after the raid. My biggest problem was to get some sleep. After an awful night I didn't feel fit enough to drive the van. On my rounds I would go to a shop to deliver some goods; next time there would be no shop there, just a big hole in the ground where a land mine had dropped. I knew all these people were killed. It was a depressing job, but I had to do it.

One night we drove our car about fifteen miles out of town into a lovely country lane. It was so peaceful there until the sirens went. A powerful searchlight went up in the next field from where we were parked. We sure got away from there as soon as we could as jerry would shoot at those searchlights. We heard the jerry planes overhead. We had to drive the car with just small lights on. What a frightening experience, no lights, only from the searchlights, we got away from there fast. We managed to get home to our usual shelter. Those guns nearly made one deaf.

We had nearly six year of this. Hoping and praying for one peaceful nights sleep. Most nights we slept with all our day clothes on, ready to run to the shelter. We had all our valuables packed, ready to grab and run to the shelter for safety. We always thought it was the safest place to be in an air raid, until the night one shelter got a direct hit, and it killed many people.

We sure met some funny characters in those shelters. Some were half drunk, and some were like tramps off the streets. Many people took to drink to try and calm their nerves. Oh, and the funny noises and smells. Phew! This big shelter held about four hundred people. It was a natural culvert, it had a stream running through it. There was a bridge we had to cross to get into the shelter. One night Hitler was dropping incendiary bombs, and one dropped at the entrance to the shelter causing clouds of steam to go into the shelter. Everyone panicked. Women and children were crushed as they tried to go further into the shelter towards all the bunk beds where people were sleeping. I was on a top bunk and the crowd just pushed all the bunks on top of each other. The screams were terrible. I just prayed for help. I thought it was my last hour. These people thought it was a gas bomb that had been dropped, that caused the panic. After a night like this I swore I'd move to where my son was, but I had a job to do. He had moved from the farm and was now living in Keswick in the Lake District of Cumberland.

Every day we used to listen to an announcer's voice on the radio, "Germany calling, Germany calling." It was James Joyce, we called him Lord Haw Haw, warning us that jerry planes would be over a certain place that night, and it would happen. He had an Oxford accent. He would warn us that Hitler would soon be living in Buckingham Palace, anything to try to frighten us. He was English and was executed at the end of the war.

One night after the sirens had gone, we grabbed all we could carry, a flask of tea and sandwiches. We got used to running in the blackout, we knew the way even without lights to this shelter. On the way we passed a high wall, about six feet. We heard a jerry plane diving, and firing his guns. We fell to the ground on our stomachs so we didn't get hit. What a lucky night. The day after we saw the holes in the wall where the bullets had gone. That same night jerry had hit the railway goods yard at Manors where tons of sugar was stored. It went up in a big blaze, and then all the flies came. People were walking around with flies on their faces for days afterwards.

We used to get so frustrated we didn't know what to do to get a good nights sleep. The guns were all around us. That caused many people to go temporarily deaf. I still had to work. I loved it, but I was feeling so very tired with the raids and an alcoholic to look after. I decided I couldn't take any more of this life. I sold all my furniture and a beautiful green carpet I had bought just a few weeks before. Nothing mattered to me any more.

I went to live with my son in Keswick. People used to call it the yellow country, where people went to get away from Hitler's bombs. I took an apartment there. It was wonderful to have my son with me again, and a good night's sleep most every night. We would get an odd jerry plane over, and he would drop his bombs anywhere when our planes were chasing him. Some farms got bombed out.

My husband went to live with a woman who had four children. I didn't see him for a while. I got a job in a grocer's shop. I met some nice people. I met a girl of my own age and she had troubles like mine, so we became good friends. She was called Betty. We would visit the pubs. There was nothing else to do at night but go to the pubs for company. We didn't drink much.

One night in the pub there were about thirty Irish soldiers. They were getting a bit too happy and started to sing Irish songs. "When Irish eyes are smiling"" etc. Everyone had tears in their eyes, and we both cried with them. They were going on manoeuvres, making a landing in the next day or so. They were all good looking boys. My heart ached for them. I believed only a small number of them ever came back to live their lives, I would think of my son and prayed to God he would never have to go to fight anyone. I don't believe in wars. Who does? After all from what I've seen, it doesn't make sense. The last war was going to be the war to end all wars. I doubt it.

Betty and I became very close friends. We needed each other. I was feeling more content now that I had my son with me and he was happy in school here. Keswick was full of military. Some nights Betty and I would go to the local dance hall instead of going to the pubs. Some nights later we met two Canadian officers. They were fine looking men in their uniforms. These uniforms were always a big attraction for me. Betty and I enjoyed many nights out with these two Canadians. They were stationed in Keswick for nearly three months, so we really got to know them. Bill was a very frank kind of person. He would tell me his troubles, and I listened with compassion to his tales of woe and tried to understand him. It was difficult at times.

He had something that attracted me to him for some reason I couldn't quite understand. He was a lovable man and expected it in return. He would listen to my troubles, but would criticise me for putting up with such behaviour from my husband. Bill confessed to many things I didn't agree with. This was something I couldn't accept. He said he loved me and couldn't live without me, but I couldn't say the same for him. He was to me a nice fellow and I kept him at bay. I felt I didn't want to get involved in a love affair like this. He had a wife and daughter in Canada. I loved my son too much to ever think of leaving him to live with another man, much as I needed the love and affection that Bill could give me. Bill was very determined that I should go back to Canada to live with him. He gave me one weekend to decide 'yes' or 'no'. I knew then what my answer would be, but I had three days to decide.

I was to see him in our usual pub on Monday evening. He would be there for my answer. Strangely enough, my husband turned up that very weekend to tell me he had got a very good job with the government, and he wanted to know if I would go back to him. We would move to another part of the country where it was safer, away from the bombings. It was a town called Alnwick, not far from the coast. I had to decide that weekend.

I went to bed early, to pray about my decision, asking God for guidance. In the morning I had the answer for both men. I decided I would try again, and take my son back with me. We didn't leave for a week. Now I had to meet Bill. I was scared what he would do or think about me refusing to go to live with him in Canada. I was not looking forward to meeting him. He would be in the pub at seven, waiting for my answer. There was no way I could get out of this situation.

Monday evening came far too quickly for me. I went to the pub as arranged at seven o'clock. I looked around, but Bill wasn't there. I really got into a panic. Where is he? This was an important date. He just couldn't miss being there on time. I waited for half an hour. No

Bill. It was really worrying me, so I left the pub and started to walk home. Just then another Canadian came up to me and asked, "Are you Pat?"

"Yes, that's me."

"I have a message for you. Bill has been transferred to an emergency battalion to go overseas on a secret mission. No on knows where he has gone."

Well, was that a relief to me! He couldn't tell me anything more than that Bill was transferred. He could see I was in a state of shock. He asked me to go back to the pub and have a drink with him. I did so.

I sure needed a drink. I wondered if that was the true story. I had to believe him. He gave me one of Bill's badges to keep in remembrance of Bill. He walked home with me and said, "Don't worry too much Pat. Bill will look after himself." To me that sounded like he was happy for me that Bill couldn't turn up to say goodbye to me.

I went to bed and slept all night with no dreams about Bill. He had gone out of my life for ever. I was looking forward to going to live in Alnwick. It was a nice quiet place, but full of history. I said goodbye to Betty, remembering all the fun we had, and now Keswick was all forgotten. Bill was a past memory. I was thankful that I didn't have to face Bill with a 'no'.

A week later we arrived in Alnwick. My husband had got us a small furnished house and we settled down. for many weeks he wasn't drinking as heavily and life seemed to be more comfortable now. I told Bill's friend that I was going to live in Alnwick and if ever he got up there, I would like to see him. I told him the name of the pub we would visit in Alnwick, but I don't think he would ever be stationed near there. There were quite a number of soldiers and airmen stationed Just outside the town.

Months went by and my husband started drinking heavily again. He was lucky to keep his job, but he did. The years seemed to pass so quickly. My son was twelve years old now and was more understanding as regards his father's drinking habit. He was a forgiving boy, and felt sorry for him. He would never take side between his father and me. He would say, "Mother, it's your problem. It's up to you to do something about it." I knew he was right.

Being born in the USA, I got a letter from the US government. When I opened it, to my surprise it had my calling up papers. I had to register to join the forces by a certain date. Well, I sure was surprised, but I thought that now this is my opportunity to get back to my birthplace. It gave me the biggest thrill of me life. Just the thought of returning to the US was like God's gift to me. I didn't tell my husband but kept the date to see the American recruiting officer. I had in mind if I could get my son into an American army cadet school, then we could both get to America one day. But that didn't work out. My son was born in England, that was the problem. They couldn't accept him, so I decided I wouldn't join the US forces. I couldn't leave my son, so that was a reasonable answer for the recruiting officer. Another dream had gone again for me. I once wrote to a well known film star in Hollywood and offered my services free to her, to pay for our fares to California. I didn't even get a reply.

I liked living in Alnwick. It was quiet, and surrounded by lovely countryside. There was not much to do, only visit the pubs. I was out shopping one afternoon and I met a girl who was working in the place where I was shopping. We seemed to have much in common. I met her several times. She was another Betty who had many problems. We became very fond of each other. I had started sewing again as we needed the money. My husband kept most of his wages for drinking. I made quite a bit of money. I worked real hard at that sewing machine. Betty was the answer to my need for pleasure. We would laugh and cry together at times.

This country town was growing on me. I enjoyed the lively walks Betty and I used to take during daylight hours. Then in the evenings we would spend a few hours a week in the local pubs. That was the only thing to do here. All the locals would get together to share problems and happy times. They were lovely people. I knew most of them by name.

Betty did some voluntary work for a military snack bar on a base nearby. There was going to be a military ball to be held in Alnwick castle. It was by invitation only. Betty was very fortunate to get two tickets. It was being held in two weeks time, so we got busy, and I made two lovely long dresses. Mine was a pretty blue and Betty's was red. We were now all set for this beautiful occasion, this once in a lifetime affair.

One of the officers picked us up and we arrived at the castle dressed to kill with long white gloves. We both must have looked very attractive. We were young and full of love, I guess. Betty had a wonderful sense of humour, like myself. We could laugh at anything. The castle grounds were just beautiful. As we arrived the moon was just coming out to the full. Once I used to hate that moon because I knew my husband would get hopelessly drunk. I am sure he was affected by the full moon. Not me. I was living in another world that night.

On entering the castle, we were greeted by the Duke and Duchess. She was a beautiful lady. The lights in the ballroom were on full, and the band struck up to play the different national anthems. There were high ranking officers from all over the world. Czechs, Australians, Americans, French and Belgians, as well as English, Scots and Welsh. I can't remember them all. Some of them only spoke broken English. That was hard to understand sometimes. These brave men were all in their full dress uniforms. I can't describe the beauty of it all. Their medals were shining as the lights went through different colours.

After all the anthems had been played, the band started to play for dancing. They started off with a Viennese waltz. The Duke and Duchess took the floor to lead the waltz. This was a beautiful sight. The Duchess wore a floor length gown which she held at her wrist as she waltzed around the room. Her jewels were sparkling in the colourful lights. The Duke's full dress uniform and medals added to his manly figure. He looked a handsome man. As the dances proceeded, they had a 'change partners' dance. I was lucky. I had a dance with the Duke. He was a beautiful dancer. I got the greatest thrill of my life.

This was a dream come true for Martha, father's last joke, dancing with a Duke!

I didn't miss many dances all evening. My next dance was with a Free French officer. He spoke broken English. It was difficult for me to understand him at times, so I was slow to answer him. I didn't want to say 'yes' when it should have been 'no'. There several intervals during the evening. Most everyone would walk in the grounds of the castle. It was such a beautiful night, and so peaceful. With the moon at full, it made it more romantic for me. I danced with many different nationalities, and walked around the castle grounds with several of them. They all proved to be perfect gentlemen. These were men a long way from home, and were prepared to give their lives for peace. What could I give these men in return? That thought came to me many times as we walked around the grounds of the castle. I felt full of admiration for these men, and the champagne was changing my personality. I was full of love. I was prepared to give my all to a man, but I was never propositioned once. That surprised me. I felt like the girl who took her harp to a party but no one asked her to play.

I had some very interesting talks with these men. They all seemed to want to talk about their problems with their wives. I was always a good listener. Jean, the Free French man, had a blind boy born to his first wife. He told me his second wife was a jewel to him. She was bringing up that boy as her own son. Pete was an Australian. He was still not married, in his thirties. He confessed he had lived with another man for three years and this was his greatest regret. I was surprised to hear this. He was such a fine looking man. I told him one day he would meet the right woman in his life, and he would marry her.

On a 'Ladies choice' dance, I picked an American Air Force officer. We did walk around the grounds, with no problems. I was surprised as I had met several Americans and they were always straight to the point. They wouldn't waste any time if you refused any of their requests. I think all these men had been put on heir best behaviour, being amongst this high society.

Then there was Jim. He had been divorced twice. He looked to me to be about in his forties. He had no children. That was his problem, he was not able to give any woman a child. I felt sorry for him. He was British. One of these men told me a story about his first wife who had fallen for a coloured man. He was still in love with her and was trying to get her to come back to him. I advised him to stay with the wife he had at the time, but I guess love must conquer all.

These confessions and stories made me think of my own problems. I didn't have time to relate them. Why spoil a beautiful night with my problems? I was living in a dream and didn't want to spoil it with my troubles.

After each dance we would make our way to the bar for more champagne and caviar. It was delicious food, even though there was a war on, and there was food rationing. Everyone was in a happy mood. The dance continued till two a.m. I didn't see much of Betty. She must have had lots of dance partners as she was a good dancer and full of fun. I didn't think Betty would part with much.

Later in the evening I met a real charmer. After a dance we sat in a lounge. He told me his name was Peter and I must call him Pete. He was different from all the others I had met there, a very different personality. I could tell he was a Scot, wearing the Highland Dress uniform. He had an Oxford accent. I asked him a few questions regarding this. Born in Scotland, he had been brought up in England, but he always wanted to be a Scotsman. We got on really well together. The fact was, sex didn't enter into our conversation at all.

It seemed to me that sex wasn't his greatest aim in life, but he was so young I couldn't understand it. He told me he had never been married. Said he had not yet met the 'Mrs. Right' for him. He talked about his family and his mother, who he said was always the first lady in his life. He went on to talk about some charming fellow he had met when he was stationed overseas. He kept on repeating how they were very close. My mind started to wander a little. What was he trying to tell me? Oh, no! I couldn't believe it. I noticed in the light of the moon that he had tears in his eyes. I touched his hand and said, "You can tell me. I'll listen to your problems." Gosh, this was something I never expected.

He cried like a baby, and told me he had lived with this fellow for two years. He was trying to forget him, but found it very difficult. He told me that once a man had practiced homosexuality, he couldn't give it up easily. I tried to convince him this was not true. "You will meet 'Mrs. Right' one of these days and have a happy married life. So you have to change your thinking habits." He thanked me for listening and we went back to dance.

Just then they were having 'The Lancers', I joined in, and at the end of the dance we all changed partners and waltzed around the room. I was fortunate enough to dance once again with the Duke. He was a handsome man. His uniform was of a Colonel, he had lots of ribbons and medals across his chest. This was a great thrill for me.

I went to find Betty as I had not seen much of her all evening. She was with a very fine looking English officer. She introduced me to him and as we talked, his friend came along, an English Navy Captain. He asked me for a dance. He was a good dancer too, although much older than I. He had that high society air about him, an 'English Gentleman', and with an Oxford accent. I had to play down my accent and not talk too much as I had been educated 'on the college walls', and had left school at age twelve. But that didn't seem to cause any problems between us. I was much younger than he. Perhaps he felt flattered to be dancing with a much younger person like me. He took me to the bar to have champagne and a snack. It was now about one a.m. The dance would be over at two. They had got a special permit as everywhere else was closed by midnight.

After a dance with this older man, I felt I didn't need him, so I made an excuse to go to the ladies room, and lost him. What an evening of surprises, but the best was yet to come. I was sitting on a lounger relaxing when someone came and sat next to me. His uniform attracted me. I just smiled my sweetest smile as the champagne was still with me. I felt like a princess. The world belonged to me again, whoever could take it from me? He smiled back at me and, to my great surprise said, "Hello mother." Mother? I thought. That sure rang a bell for me, as my husband always called me 'mother'. I tried to think where he came in. It must be a connection with me husband in some way. I just couldn't bring to mind who he was. He was a charming fellow in his thirties. He asked me for a dance. The feeling I got wasn't too good. He must know my husband.

The champagne was wearing off by now. It suddenly hit me who he was. Oh, my goodness, no not him, I thought. But it was. He was the fellow who brought my husband home some weeks ago. They were both drunk. I remember that night, I had to put both men to bed. He had been in civilian clothes and he had a moustache I'm sure of that. I also remember he was called Jack. I had sat up most of the night too scared to go to bed. It got to three o'clock in the morning and Jack walked into the sitting room where I was trying to get some sleep. It shocked me to see he was naked. He came over to me and a struggle started. It was like a fight for life. I was really in a state of panic. I didn't know what to do next. I grabbed a table lamp and hit him with it. He was out for the count. I thought I'd killed him. He lay there till morning. My husband slept through it all. At seven o'clock he woke up, went to the bedroom, dressed and came down to apologise to me. I told him I was sorry I'd hit him with the lamp, but he asked for it. And this was the fellow I was dancing with! I noticed the scar on his forehead, which must have been from where the lamp hit him. I got away from him as quickly as possible when I realised who he was.

It was now about one forty five and the last waltz was going to be played soon. That usually means the fellow who picks you for the last waltz takes you home. Just then Betty turned up again. She had another fellow with her. He was a real good looker. He was another Scot. Their Dress uniforms make them look so attractive. They went off to dance the last waltz. There I was just standing there and wondering who was going to be the next partner to dance with. No one came, and the dance was nearly over. I was feeling tired and wasn't interested in the last waltz. I decided to go to the cloakroom when a fellow came up behind me and said, "Oh, you aren't going home yet. Please let's dance."

Before I knew it, I was in his arms dancing to the tune of my favourite song, 'Three o'clock in the morning'. This seemed like the beautiful end of a dream come true for me. This could never happen to me again, and for a lot of the other people who were there. It only happens once in a lifetime. This is something I shall never forget. I believe God did guide me to Alnwick. I always ask Him for guidance and I rely on Him.

The last waltz was over, and he offered to take me home. He said he had an army vehicle and did I mind riding in a truck? It turned out to be a car, not a truck, but I had already accepted a lift home. We found Betty and her friend, and of we went. We didn't get home as soon as we expected. They took us around to their barracks about three miles away. It seems these men knew each other. They were from the same barracks. We talked, and had tea and coffee. The barracks was still alive with people around. We felt quite safe there.

We had just decided to leave for home when the sirens went. We could hear the jerry bombers overhead, and we all rushed to the shelter. We heard the guns and could tell that some bombs had been dropped not far from here. It was most unusual to have a raid when the moon was full, as they could be seen coming in the distance. But they had come over in strength. The only thing I could think of was the safety of my son. He was living in a boarding school a few miles out of Alnwick. At last the 'all clear' went about four o'clock and we made for home. Those two fellows were wonderful to us. When I got home. my husband was sound asleep. I guess he'd had too much to drink, went to sleep and didn't hear anything. Lucky man. It was nearly five o'clock before I went to sleep. I lay there in bewilderment. Could it have been little ol' me dancing with a Duke? I fell asleep in his arms, to dream again.

Betty and I attended another dance at the castle, but that one was not all military. Some Canadian soldiers were there and got too much to drink and started to pull the animals heads off the walls. The Duke closed the castle for dances after that. I was sorry about that. Too much drinking can change a man's personality. I know it does with me. When I take more than two drinks, I'd give anything away. My mother gave me the best advice, "Always keep both feet on one brick love, and you can't lose."

I guess she didn't use that brick much herself, eight children in ten years. She used to say that if my father only hung his trouser on the bedpost she would get pregnant! In those days they all had big families, father promised there would be no more babies after me.

Chapter Three.

We lived in Alnwick till the end of the war, then moved back to Newcastle upon Tyne. We took a middle floor furnished flat not far from the city centre. Above us lived an elderly man, I'd call him old. He must have been over sixty. We didn't know his business. We would see him going out with his black bag. I used to wonder what was in that bag. We found out later that he was known to many as 'Dr Pot Joy'. All the prostitutes knew him. He would visit these women's flats to perform abortions. He carried the tools of his trade in that black bag, and used it to carry away the unwanted babies. It seems he had been a Doctor, but had been crossed off the register for some wrong practices.

One evening we were sitting quietly when we heard loud screams coming from upstairs. Then a shot was fired. We both ran upstairs to find the doctor lying dead and a young man standing over him. Apparently this doctor had performed an operation on this young man's wife and she had died. This was very upsetting for me. I felt I couldn't stay in this apartment, so we decided to move to another part of town. My husband was not drinking too much now. He would sometimes go for two weeks without getting hopelessly drunk.

We met a Scottish couple who travelled up to Glasgow once a month. She invited me to go with them for two nights. I found out on that trip they were heavy drinkers. They knew how to drink Scotch whiskey and not get too drunk. They would drink a pint of milk, then take a tablespoon of olive oil before they started out on a drinking spree. It seems the whiskey floated on top of the oil and they didn't get drunk.

New Years Eve in Glasgow is a terrible place. It was always a tragic night for someone. I did hear one story, I don't know if it's true, but funny, I thought. It happened in one of those high apartment buildings. Some are six or more stories high, a flat on each floor. There was a drunken man going up the stone stairs. He met another drunk coming down. The one coming down said, "Hey pal. Just be careful when you get up there. They have two cases of venereal."

"Och," the other replied, "I can drink anything tonight." Could be, I thought.

Some people say the Scots are mean. I have never met one in my life that was mean, that was not true. They used to say though, If ever you meet a good Welshman, shoot him before he goes bad. But I consider that there good and bad in all people.

I was only away from home for two nights. I got a shock when I arrived home from Scotland. My husband had an accident and was rushed to hospital. His car was smashed to pieces. I went to see him at the hospital. He was unrecognisable. The doctor told me they expected he wouldn't live through the night. They advised me to do home and they would let me know how he was later, but they didn't give me much hope. To me I had very mixed feelings. I had put up with his drinking bouts for fifteen years I just felt I couldn't take it much longer. I prayed for him and left him in God's hands. He lived through that night, and the next, and the next. Yes, he was going to live, they thought, to be a vegetable. I didn't question God. I knew I could take it with his help. He was in hospital for ten weeks and the doctors were pleased with his condition. They said he was much better than they had ever hoped he would be, but he would be in a wheel chair the rest of his life.

When he came home he would get depressed often. He wasn't drinking much now. We couldn't afford it. I now wondered which was the worst, a drunk or a helpless man to look after all day and night. I tried to do some sewing for some people I had met at the hospital. Months went by and it was a terrible ordeal for both of us. I felt I just had to get out of that house or I'd die. So I took a job at a very good class local pub, working nights only. I did enjoy the company, it helped me to keep sane. Everything seemed to work out fine for my husband. He had a neighbour who would come in and play cards with him. I was so grateful for that kindness.

I was enjoying the hotel life again meeting all kinds of characters. This was a good class hotel and we got the upper class visiting us. I liked that, I always tried to look up. Christmas was coming and every place was decorated with bright lights, and the pub would be packed with people. This is what I needed so badly, someone to talk to, someone to tell me their problems and this was the right place to be for all that. I was loving it more every night. I met some fine people, mostly men. Christmas came. This was the time to be joyful. Everyone seemed happy. I got plenty of attention and many offers, not marriage yet, but just to have fun and free love. I soon informed these men that they were talking to the wrong gal. Of course, some had too much to drink, and they were not responsible for saying many things. These tempting offers would come from some married men, and I had met their wives. They would give me that old line, "My wife doesn't understand me."

I'd tell them, "Neither do I."

Christmas Eve turned out to be a very memorable night for me. I met a real Mr Charmer, and he was single. He was in his thirties, a little younger than I, but I know, at that time I didn't look my age. I had turned blonde just the week before and I think that did something to attract men. As my husband's women were all blondes, maybe I should have gone blonde the first year I married him. But he was furious when he saw I was blonde. I wonder if it does prove to be true, only blondes go to Paris? I'll take a chance. Why not? What am I saving it for?

The hotel was packed with people. I had so many invitations out for dinner, but I couldn't accept them. I had an invalid at home to care for. I often wondered for how long. It had been six months now since he came home. Henry's full name was Henry William Armstrong. Now here was Mr Charmer in my life again. He said he had never married. I don't know how he escaped it, as he was such a good looking man and looked very prosperous. I tried not to let my thoughts wander, but the past experiences I'd had came to my mind. I hoped I was wrong. He would bring me home after the pub was closed. We would just sit in his car and talk. We seemed to have so much to talk about. I told him my problems, but he didn't seem to want to talk much of his.

I had known Henry now for three months and we had grown very close. I had to admit I was in love with him, but knew I could not tell him so. He would sometimes talk of marriage, but that was as far we could go. One evening as he brought me home there was an ambulance and a police car outside my home. Henry came with me to see what was wrong. My husband had fallen and hit his head on a stone step. He had tried to walk. They were taking him to hospital. Just half an hour later I got a call from the hospital saying my husband had died of a brain haemorrhage. Well, that was a shock for me, but I took it as a great relief. The thought of living alone didn't concern me any more.

I kept on working at the pub. It helped me a great deal and Henry was there every night to take me home. He became a blessing to me. He would come in my apartment for a cuppa most nights. We would talk about me, but Henry didn't seem to want to get involved in talking about himself. I was feeling more suspicious than before. What is on his mind? "Henry", I said, "you can talk to me, I will understand. Please be honest with me. I can take it."

The first surprise was, his mother, with whom he was living, was a Quaker. I had met her once and she seemed to be a lovely person. I understand Quakers don't believe in wars, and she was very much against Henry going to fight in a war.

He was very loyal to his country and had joined the Air Force as a rear gunner. Those boys didn't have much chance of survival. When his plane was hit, they had to crash land on enemy territory, in France, where he was picked up for dead. He was really broken up, body and soul.

He would sometimes start to talk about us getting married, as there were no problems where I was concerned. But it was Henry. Was it his mother who didn't want us to marry? Yet she seemed to like me. He would repeat and repeat to me that he loved me more than words could say. So what was stopping him from getting married? We talked into the early hours of the morning. "Pat, I don't know how I'm going to tell you this..." I assured him again and again that I would understand. I noticed that he had tears in his eyes. He held my hand so tightly, he almost hurt me. He was crying then. ""Pat, I can't marry you. Please understand."

Well. There goes my dream again, "Why not Henry. Why? Why? Tell me the truth." He went on to say he was no use to me. I should let him go. "But Henry. You know I love you." I was crying now. I was shaking with emotion. I just couldn't wait any longer to find out what was worrying him. I thought then, perhaps it was something physical that was not normal with him. I did know he had some serious wounds in his body, but where I did not know.

"Pat darling, you know I love you and I'll make you the happiest woman alive if you will marry me just as I am." Henry was shot up around his manhood and he had nothing to offer a woman. I believe they used to call it D.S.O. That could mean different kinds of disability. This was a shock to me. I never gave that kind of disability a thought.

So, now. Where do I go from here? How can Henry make me the happiest woman without the love I need so badly? I had not had any sexual love for years. I told him how sorry and sad I was to hear his pathetic story. I tried to comfort him by saying that having sex doesn't always bring happiness, but it does help. He agreed with me, and he just hugged and kissed me until I was breathless. I couldn't answer him. I was still happy to work at the pub. It was a great help to me to talk to different people and listen to their problems. Then mine seemed so small.

Henry would come in every night and take me home. He would come in for an hour or so, but he wasn't pushing me for an answer to his proposal of marriage, so I didn't say much regarding such a marriage. I loved him. I felt I just couldn't live without him, but could I take that kind of marriage? Should I try? It kind of scared me as I am a very affectionate person. I need a lot of loving. I knew this was worrying Henry. He had told me his greatest secret. Would he be happy under those circumstances?

As the weeks went by he became more precious to me. I felt I couldn't let him down. He had to stay in my life. This had to be my decision.

I married him three weeks later. Henry didn't want to tell his mother he had married. He kept that from her. He went on living at his mother's house. I didn't like that arrangement. We had been married nearly four months and he still hadn't told his mother he had married. I would see her often and was tempted many times to tell her, but Henry said it would break her heart. She thought it was hopeless for him to marry, knowing he could not have any children, or a normal life with any woman.

We had no financial worries as Henry had a good job, and a good pension. Also his father had left him an income for life. He used to beg me to give up working at the pub, but I needed that company. All this secrecy was making me very unsettles in my thought world. I had started to think this was all wrong and I didn't think I could take this kind of arrangement. I was hoping that Henry could change.

I got a letter from a dear friend, Claire, whom I had known for many years. She told me she had just lost her husband with a heart attack and she was feeling so lonely. She asked if I would go and stay with her for a few weeks. She didn't know I had remarried. But I though, what a wonderful idea of hers. I'd love it. She lived in Manchester, where I used to live. I met her there many years ago. She was my bridesmaid at my wedding, when I was first married in Manchester Cathedral, but I hadn't heard from her for quite a while.

Chapter Four.

I decided to go and see her. I told Henry It was only for a short while, but my intentions were different. I felt I couldn't take any more of this life with him, much as I loved him. I had the marriage annulled. It was a hopeless marriage. I had let my heart rule my brain, and it didn't work that way. I didn't give Henry my address where I was staying. I didn't want to hear or see him any more. I knew I would miss him as he was so kind to me in other ways.

Claire and I became very close friends. She needed me and I needed her. We both got jobs in the same hotel. She worked in the snack bar and I worked at the beer bar. We enjoyed each other's company.

This hotel was quite near to where my parents had a hotel before I married. I recognised some of the customers who used to be in our pub years ago. They were surprised and delighted to see me again, but they brought back unhappy memories for me. I wasn't very happy to talk to them about my past. They would ask too many personal questions. I told Claire I didn't think I liked working there. I would like to move on to London where no one knew me. I'd like a new start in life. Claire was disappointed, but I left for London.

I looked up an old girl friend I had not seen for years. She lived in the same house. I was lucky I found her in as she had a very busy schedule. She was a private secretary to a lawyer. She invited me to stay with her until I got settled in some where. She had a very nice furnished flat, just about a mile from Piccadilly. I remembered her name so well, she was called Mary Winterbottom. She had never married and still used the same name. I guess she had too good a job to give up for married life.

Mary introduced me to a married couple who managed a private hotel just two streets away from where we lived. I got a job helping them during the day for a few hours, and got another job in a hotel in the same area. I liked the evening work in the pub. They were a very mixed crowd. The manager was in his fifties. We got on together very well. I worked three nights a week. He asked me if I would like to live in the hotel like some of his employees did. I thought that was a good idea, so I moved in and did a full time job. This suited me better, and Mary was happy about this. She knew I had spent many years in the hotel business and that was where I belonged, so I settled down there.

Henry was someone who had just passed out of my life for good. I had not the time to even think of him any more. London was a beautiful place to me. I realised this is where I should stay. This pub was close to everything, shops and shows. Yes, and Ascot wasn't too far away. I knew I was going to be happy here. I met some real strange characters. Some were very talented. The Opera House was near here. Some folks would drop in for drinks before the show, and at the intervals. In those days they had no bars in the theatre. I got quite a thrill to se all the men dressed in cloaks and top hats, and the ladies in long gowns with flowers in their bosoms, sparkling with diamonds, fur coats, and long gloves to match. It was fascinating to see them. I hoped one day I'd be with them.

When I went to shows I would queue for two hours to get a seat in the gallery. We had to walk up five flights of stone steps to get to our seats. We saw ballet, The Merry Widow, and other operas. A long climb, but Oh, it was worth while. It was a great thrill for me. I had a visit from my son. I hadn't seen him for three years. He surely had grown into a fine looking man. He had married and settled down, living in the northeast of England. I was hoping he would come to live with me. I didn't know he had married. I had planned many things we would do together, but his wife would come first now.

One evening the manager and his wife went to the opera. They left me in charge of the bar. We had three waiters, and I thought they were honest men, but they took advantage of me being in charge. We had the busiest night. I didn't know where all the people came from. We heard later that the hotel down the street had been raided for some reason and was closed. The police in plain clothes would make an unexpected visit and close the pub for different reasons. Some dark characters would be picked up and jailed. So we got the overflow from that pub.

We were so busy, one of our customers offered to help me. He turned out to be a greater help to himself. He got away with £100 that night. He knew the boss wasn't there to watch him, and the temptation was too great for him. I was very upset about this, but the manager was very kind and considerate to me. He understood my position.

Talking about temptation, I've had plenty. A fellow came into the pub and offered me a packet of money if I would just sign a slip. He was what they called a runner for a bookie, one who takes bets. His boss was at the races that day and he asked me if I wanted to make an easy £50. Was that temptation for me?! The horse was called Turkey

Buzzard. It had run, and won, at 20 to 1 in the two o'clock race. I didn't know this. "Sign this Pat, and I'll give you fifty quid, it's a sure winner." Well. Should I or should I not? That £50 would be very welcome. I walked away to serve a customer and my dear father's words came back to me, 'Honesty is the best policy'. I went back to him and told him to 'B' off. I was too busy working for money. He was shocked that I had refused him. This is one of the kind of people you meet in pubs.

I was feeling unsettled again. I read an advertisement in the evening paper for a manageress for a private hotel in Bournemouth, by the sea and just one hour from London. I wrote and got an interview, and got the job. They gave me a lovely furnished flat overlooking the ocean. This was heaven for me to watch the waves roll in. It gave me a feeling of security to have my own flat. This private hotel had ten bedroom but only two bathrooms.

I had some very good helpers. That was my biggest headache, to get the right type of person. I used to advertise for help now and then, as many of them were not reliable. We had a man to do the yard work etc. He was alright sometimes, but he liked his whiskey. He couldn't hold his liquor. One night, late, I got a call from the police. He was locked up for disturbing the peace on the promenade. He was a real oddball. His wife had left him years ago. He used to tell me about all the jobs he'd had. One time he was a grave digger, and was responsible for the upkeep of a small cemetery. He had the keys to open the main gate when he needed to. He said he made quite a bit of money in the evenings charging local prostitutes one pound a time for the use of the cemetery. I had never heard of a thing like that to happen in a graveyard. That must have been a case of stone cold reality on those stone tables.

I got rid of him. He was not reliable. I advertised in the paper for a man helper. I got an answer in a letter that was badly written, but somehow it appealed to me. He sounded like a worker. He was to arrive at ten a.m. for an interview with me. He arrived at nine. He sat in the waiting room off the hallway. When he walked in I was shocked beyond words. I looked carefully at him, and thought I knew him. His hair was nearly white. He was a short and tubby little man.

When he spoke to me. My goodness! No! It can't be Joe who I knew years ago. He was the fellow who had helped me move furniture around the house, and was always helpful when I had to bail my husband out of jail. I was sure it was him, but he didn't recognise me at first. I had dark hair when he knew me, now he was being interviewed by a blonde. I smiled at him and said, "Don't you know me Joe?"

He looked at me and said, "Oh. Aren't you the lady who said I stole her handbag last year?" I started to think, what's this I hear, Joe stealing a ladies handbag? No. I can't believe that. Not the Joe I knew. "Oh," He said, "But that was a mistaken identity. It wasn't me who stole the ladies handbag." Gosh, that was a relief. He still didn't recognise me, so I had to remind him who I was. He couldn't believe it. He had tears in his eyes. "Pat, you look wonderful." He asked me all kinds of questions, where, and who, but I told him it was too long a story to relate it now. Joe, I remembered, had a pension from the army. He was badly shot up, and it seemed his memory was failing too.

The interview was over, and we arranged that he would start in the morning. I asked him if he wanted to live in, or did he have a room somewhere. He told me he was living alone in a one bed roomed flat. "Joe, what happened to the widow you were living with when I knew you?"

"Oh," He said, "she died a tragic death. She was murdered."

"Murdered!" I said, "by whom?"

"Pat, that case went on for over a year and I was in jail for all that time pending the result. I had no part in that murder. It was proved that it was her late boy friend she had left to come and live with me. He got life imprisonment for it."

"Joe, I can't believe it's you. We have talked too long. Be here at 8 in the morning and I will give you your duties then."

Joe arrived before eight and began sweeping the leaves from the pathway. Joe wasn't the same fellow when I knew him years ago. He must have gone through many hard times. He was much slower than I remember, but he had kept his sense of humour. As weeks went by, I didn't offer him a room in the hotel. Something told me not to. Let him keep his own accommodation away from me. Joe must be in his fifties now.

One day he brought along a young lad about eighteen. He introduced him to me as his son. I said, "I didn't know you had any children."

"Yes. I had three with my first wife." His son was a good looker, he looked like Joe. To me it seemed strange that this boy would turn up later in Joe's life. Somehow, I doubted Joe. Well, I wasn't concerned about that as long as Joe did the work right. I didn't want to probe into his life. I might get a few shocks.

Joe was a good worker. Everything went well. He had been with me nearly a year now. All my helpers were good. I had a chambermaid who was friendly with Joe. He would ask me about my past experiences. I told him a few. He would laugh and say, "Pat, you will never change."

I enjoyed managing this hotel. We had some very interesting people who stayed for a long weekend. Some were retired and once in a while we would have an elderly gentleman with a young blonde for the weekend. That didn't interest me, as my love life had been neglected for a period of years now. I told myself, one of these days I'd have to get back into the pub business again. That was where I met people, people who I needed. After all, life was passing me by quickly now. I had to get out and find someone to love and obey. Yes, love, but I couldn't promise to obey. They would have to take me just as I am. Pat, a lover to be loved.

I had a very good cleaning woman and a maid. They were both very dedicated women to me. I just felt I'd be letting them down if I decided to leave this management. I tried not to let my mind wander back to the pubs. It was difficult for me to do that. One day, Mary, the chambermaid, who wasn't married, confessed to me that she was expecting a baby. "Who's the fellow Mary?" I asked. She had tears in her eyes. I looked at her, and said, "Oh no. It's not Joe?" She sobbed and nodded her head. Yes. It was Joe. My God, what next?

I spoke to Joe about it and he denied it. He said, "I just couldn't give anyone a baby if I wanted to. She's out of her mind if she thinks she's going to pin that on me. She's had it. My doctor can prove it."

Well. It sounded like we were going to have trouble in the camp.. I didn't know if Joe was telling me the truth. I decided to get from under all this trouble. I gave notice to leave the management of this hotel. I had six weeks before I would leave. I didn't tell anyone I was leaving until the week before I left.

I had answered adverts for London and got a few good offers and interviews. One I was interested in, it had many sweet offers. I interviewed three, mostly in the heart of London. All seemed good class hotels. I had an appointment with one manager who seemed very nice. I got the job. It was part residential, and it had a large drinking room and three bars. I was to be in charge of one of these bars. I found it a very interesting place, lots of different kinds of people stayed there. We had some wealthy foreigners. We had wealthy Arabs who used to tip very well. I had a good job there.

I said goodbye to Joe, and said, "Come and see me one day." But this wasn't the kind of hotel Joe would visit, so I never saw him. I don't know what happened to Mary and her baby, or if she had it. I had started a new life again, I wanted to forget the past. I was enjoying this lovely hotel, and the people who came in. They were my kind of people.

Chapter Five.

It was summer time now, and it was light till way after ten. I liked to take a walk before retiring to my comfortable bed sitting room on the third floor. It was a warm August night and for the first time in my life I felt lonely. As I came to the corner of the street I saw what I thought was a little old lady selling flowers. As I got closer I saw that her face was full of wrinkles. I couldn't resist. I bought some flowers from her and gave her more money than she asked for. She gave me the sweetest smile and thanked me many times for my generosity. I stood talking to her for a while. She was an interesting person to know.

I made a practice of seeing her most nights of the week. I think she looked forward to seeing me. I did also. We seemed to have a lot in common. When I went to see her I'd be there sometimes over an hour. We talked and talked. She told me many interesting things about herself. She seemed to be filling this lonely gap I had just now. I liked to hear people's problems, it makes mine seem so small. We both had the same feelings towards each other. I remember my father saying, "You can learn from the poor, they understand life better." This to me was an example. I was drawn to this dear old lady. She needed something in life and I did my best to give it to her. I think it was love. She seemed to be a love starved person. I was feeling the same just then. My love life was very empty. I felt if someone said they loved me, I would feel much happier. This is why I was pouring my love and affection out to this love starved old lady. She used to look forward to seeing me every day. If I missed, she said she felt sad. So I made a daily or evening visit to see her.

Surprisingly enough, she was spotlessly clean. She smelt clean. Her clothes were old but clean. I once got a whiff of perfume coming from her. I had known her for several weeks now One day she invited me to visit her home. Home, I thought. I visualised she was living in one of these, what they call tramp's houses, or in a Salvation Army hostel, or a common lodging house. I couldn't believe she'd have a home of her own. I didn't like the idea of going to where she was living, as one could expect to see anything. In these lodging houses there were some dark characters. I wasn't too thrilled with the idea, but I had to go.

I had to call her Molly. I thought that suited her beautifully. I met her one evening early on my night off, and she took me to her home. We walked down two streets and I noticed some really big terraced houses, three stories high. I thought, this can't be where she lives. I remember it was the third house from the corner. She slowed up and started to fumble in the big canvas bag she always carried. She brought out a large bunch of keys. We walked up four steps to this big heavy door. As she opened it, out rushed four dogs. They were so happy to see her, all makes, mostly mongrels, but very affectionate to her, and to me. They all looked well fed.

As we walked down the lobby, or hallway, I noticed one door was open and I could see some lovely ornaments, and what looked the older style of furniture. We went through into her kitchen. It was the older type of kitchen, but she had some new equipment, a huge refrigerator etc. We sat down and she made me a cup of tea. The dogs went crazy to see her she would give them a biscuit and they would jump onto her lap and lick her face. I guess this was the only affection Molly ever got. The kitchen was spotlessly clean too. She told me she had a woman who cleaned for her twice a week and she had a gentleman who had the whole floor above her. He would take the dogs in turn for a walk, twice a day.

Now Molly knew me as Pat. We used to call each other 'love'. She gave me a tour of her ground floor flat. It was huge. Her bedrooms were at the back of the house. She had a great big bed with all the frills on it. She had some kind of patchwork cover across her bed. I was surprised to see she had a large bathroom leading off the bedroom. It was all modern, except for the bath, in the middle of the room, it was so old fashioned, but it was beautiful. It was a mixture of old and modern all through the house. She took me to her front sitting room, this was huge and packed with antiques. I noticed she had a grand piano and there were sheets of music around. I said to her, "Molly, do you play the piano?"

"I do love, I'll play you something." She sat down and started to play the very old songs my mother used to sing, such as, 'I'll take you home again Kathleen', and 'Lily of Laguna'. This brought tears to my eyes. Can this be the little old lady to whom I had given an extra shilling for the flowers I'd bought from her all those weeks ago? I couldn't believe it. How one can be mistaken!

I saw a picture once of a lady carrying a violin case getting onto a bus and the case burst open. Brown potatoes rolled out. So, things aren't always what they seem.

We continued to walk through her house. We came to another bedroom. "This is my dog's bedroom." They all had their own beds. They were fed in there too, and it was just as clean as the rest of the house. Molly had a nice singing voice. I wouldn't dare ask how old she was. Some people don't like to tell their age. To me she was young and beautiful. I think we both talked ourselves dry. "What about a cuppa tea love?"

"Molly, I'd love it." We talked all evening. She told me the story of her life. She was born in this big house. She and her brother had a nanny to care for them. There was a maid's quarters upstairs too. When she became school age, she was sent to Switzerland to a boarding school. Her brother was in college in London. They didn't see each other often, only once a year at Christmas. When Molly was seventeen, she had to leave school. To the shock of her parents, she was expecting a baby. She had been meeting, unknown to his parents, the son of a Lord and Lady who lived in England. When he told his parents of Molly's condition, he was taken away from school and was sent to Australia on a farm. That was the last Molly saw of him. Molly came home to have her baby. His people wanted to adopt the baby. Her parents thought it was a good idea, so she let them bring up their grandson. She never saw him again until years later, when he came to visit her.

Molly told me at that time her parents had an antique shop in one of London's malls. She would help them occasionally. They also had a flower shop nearby, selling flowers that came from all over the world. Molly had a fascination for flowers all her life after that. It was twenty five when she met a man who had a beautiful garden, nothing but flowers. They became very close, but never married.

Molly was growing away from her parent's shop, and started a new florist shop in the mall with this man friend. They made a very prosperous business together. They a joint agreement that if he died it would become Molly's shop. Many years passed and that business became too big for two people to manage, so they got a manager in to help. Molly was then in her thirties when Jim, her partner in the business, suddenly died and that left Molly with the shop. That became too big a responsibility for her, so she sold out and went back to helping her parents in their antique shop.

When she was forty, her parents died in a shocking tragedy. They had taken a cruise to America on the Titanic. It, and Molly's parents were lost at sea. they were never found. Her brother, who was married and living in Paris, Came home to take over the responsibilities of the shop. Molly was not fit to do anything. She had a nervous breakdown, and was in a semi mental home for five years. She was a very sick woman. She told me she couldn't remember the time she had been in this home. It had been a nightmare to her.

When she came home, she wasn't the same person. "Pat, I would never tell anyone this. Only you." She was very attached to me. We seemed to know each other's thoughts and ways of life. She was still a sick woman. She had a nurse to live in and look after her. She used to walk the streets in a daze and once was picked up by the police because they thought she was drunk. She was taken home by ambulance. It took her a few years to get back to normal.

Molly didn't see much of her brother, or his wife. They were busy at the shop, and socialising at lots of parties. They got tired of looking after the shop, and decided to sell it. But when their parent's will was read, the brother got a shock as Molly got most everything. Three houses at the coast which were rented out, the house she lived in, and that prosperous business. Her parents knew that her brother did not need anything. He was a wealthy man, and had married into wealth too. So now Molly was an independent lady.

She told me she wanted to amongst flowers again. She wanted to sell them, but not in a shop, but on a street corner. That was going to be her way of meeting people, and to get to know them. She found herself a spot, a place where she could sell flowers on the street. She could sit on a low wall with an iron railing to support her back. It was outside an old house which was due to be pulled down one day. She had been there for ten years now. People would buy from her just to be able to say, "Good morning Molly love. How are you this wonderful day?" Molly always had a sweet smile for them.

I had a wonderful evening with her. It had got very late to walk back to the hotel, so she asked me if I would like to sleep there for the night. I thanked her, but I walked to the hotel, It wasn't far. She asked me if I would come and live with her. I could keep my job at the hotel. She had many rooms and would make me comfortable. She just wanted me for company, although she had the gentleman upstairs. He would come down for a cup of tea now and then. But Molly needed me, and I had a need for her. So I moved in and I found it very comfortable and clean, it wasn't far from the pub. I didn't even have to clean my room, she had this lady to do all the cleaning right throughout the house.

I had met many nice friends at the pub now. Molly was a different person since I moved in with her. We were so happy together. I asked her once what happened to her son, and did she ever see him. No, she hadn't seen him since that first time. She did know that he had married into high society, perhaps a Lady.

I had lived with Molly for three years now. One afternoon we had a terrific thunderstorm, one of the worst I'd seen. It was as dark as night and there was terrific lightning. It scared me. I was worried about Molly sitting there in that storm. I knew she wouldn't move. She had an umbrella. I hoped God would protect her. I was very worried about her. I heard an ambulance, but I didn't attach any importance to it regarding Molly. I got the shock of my life. Molly had been struck be lightning and had been taken to hospital. I was working at the time, but I rushed over to the hospital as soon as I could. She was sleeping.

After a week they brought her home. She was a real sick Molly. Jim, the gentleman upstairs and I looked after her. I packed up the job at the pub so I could be with her. She just wanted me there all the time. I was happy to help her. Jim was a great help too. He was also quite wealthy, a retired Colonel from the British army. I guess he would have a big pension. One could see he was a gentleman in all his ways. I could recognise that. I noticed he had a limp. He told me later he had a false leg from the knee down, but it didn't stop him from walking the dogs every day. He was in his fifties, but looked much younger. We got on well together.

I got a call from the manager of the pub to ask if I could go and help them for a couple of nights. I asked Molly if I should, and she said, "It will make a change for you Pat. I'll be all right, Jim will come down and be with me." I was almost afraid to leave her as I could see she was sinking faster every day. On the second night Jim 'phoned me to tell me to come home straight away as Molly was dying. I couldn't get home fast enough. I was too late, she had died. It broke my heart that I wasn't with her when she passed on. I wanted to be with her to the end of her life. Her brother also arrived too late.

Months passed by. I was missing Molly more every day. Jim was a jewel to me. He knew how I loved Molly. I could not believe she had gone for good out of my life. Her brother came to see me one day. I didn't know why he should visit me. He wasn't very nice to me. He threw some papers on the table. It was Molly's will. He said, "You managed to get it all. Yes. You have got all Molly's money and her property." I was shocked beyond words. What the hell was he talking about?

"I don't understand all this."

"You can't kid me," he replied, "You got Molly to make her entire estate over to you. She hasn't left me one penny. It's a damn good job I don't need any from her."

I was breathless. Molly had never once talked about her possessions or her will. I had no idea she was wealthy.

That very day I got a letter from her solicitor asking me to come and see him as soon as possible. I was still shocked, my knees were trembling as I walked into the solicitors office.

"Good morning Pat. I have some good news for you." I wondered how he knew my name. He told me that Molly had made a lot of enquiries about me, and he knew my full name. I didn't know all that. Next time he called me Mrs. Armstrong, which was the name I took on my second marriage. I kept that name. He read Molly's will to me. I was flabbergasted, I couldn't take it in. It just didn't sink into my brain that I had been left all her possessions. The house I lived in and everything in it, and three houses at the coast somewhere that were rented out. Molly's lawyer was going to look after all this for me. He convinced me that Molly's brother couldn't claim a penny, not that he needed it anyway. "So, don't you worry Mrs. Armstrong, I'll look after everything for you. There will be a settlement in a few months. I'll keep in touch with you."

I was still in a dream. All this had come out of my giving an old lady an extra shilling for some flowers five years before; yet she had never told me about all that wealth. Now, where do I go from here? I realised I had become a wealthy person. I hoped it would not change my personality, because I loved people. And I had dearly loved Molly just for what she was, a flower lady.

I got really unsettled again without Molly to talk to. Maybe I should go back to work in the pub for a while. So I did for a time, just in the evenings, once or twice a week. It helped me to forget Molly.

There was only one dog left now, the others had died of old age. Jim would take it for a walk every day as usual. I wondered why Molly hadn't left Jim any money. I found out later that Jim was a very wealthy man himself, and didn't need Molly's money. Jim's wife was in high society before she died and left him a fortune.

I had never explored Molly's house before, so Jim and I went through it. I amazed at what I came across. She had money and jewellery hidden all over the house. I even found money under carpets; yes, thousands of old pound notes.

Jim often came down to see me, and would invite me up for a cup of tea. I was surprised to see he had a bachelor's type of home. I gathered he was all man in all of his ways. He had beautiful oil paintings I had never seen before, and a lot of silverware and china. He also had books by the hundreds, he was fond of reading. He had a modern grand piano in the sitting room. This was a three story house, his flat was in the middle. He gave me a tour of his flat. His bathroom was beautiful, just like Molly's. His bedroom was full of antiques, I was not then well up on the value of antiques, but I guessed they were valuable pieces.

It has amazed me since I knew Molly, how one can be mistaken. In Jim's flat alone there must have been a lot of money. He had some beautiful carpets, right throughout the flat. The bathroom had a lovely eastern carpet in front of the antique bath.

Jim was always dressed nicely, not over dressed, and he always looked like he had just stepped out of the bath tub, always with a sweet odour coming from him. This made him an attractive man to me. He told me he had a cleaning lady every day to clean his flat and cook for him.

Molly's flat was full of antiques, I hadn't looked at them all yet. I never did care for antiques, I go for all modern things. I don't know if I can live amongst them. I guess I will for a while.

Eventually I gave up my job at the pub. I would visit them occasionally as I had a strong drawing to them. It was a different atmosphere than that of Molly's house. Sometimes all this wealth became a bore to me. Antiques always reminded me of the past, and who wants to dwell in the past? I don't

Jim was a great help to me. He seemed to grow on me. He was always there when I needed him. Jim must have been in his sixties, and I was nearly forty five, so I had better hurry and live the sort of life I had always wanted to live. I had been neglected for too long.

Jim came down one morning all dressed up. He was going to the Ascot races. "Well my dear, what about it?" He never called me Pat, always dear or love.

"Jim," I replied with a sweet smile, "I just can't go today. I haven't got the clothes to wear to go to those places." I knew Jim would be taking me to the Ladies Circle, that was where Royalty would be. I was greatly thrilled with the thought of it and promised him I would go with him the day after. He must be well up in society, otherwise he wouldn't get tickets for the enclosure to the Ladies Circle. Jim reminded me the Queen and her husband would be there the next day. This made me feel like a lady. I went out and bought myself some beautiful clothes fit for a Queen to see. I was pleased with my buy.

I went to the hairdresser and she made my hair look a pretty blonde, but I would wear a hat as all the select wear hats at the races. You never see the Queen without a hat. She is a beautiful lady. It would be a great thrill for me to be near her. I could hardly wait for the next day.

Jim got home about nine o'clock. I called to him as he was about to walk up stairs, "Had any luck Jim?" That was my greeting to him.

"My dear, I hit a double and it paid plenty." Jim didn't seem too interested in money. He loved the horses and the people he would meet there. I would say they were his class of people, ones he had mixed with all his life. I was looking forward to meeting these people. Hoping I would fit in with this high society. I had always been able to rise to the occasion and I knew when to keep my mouth shut. This was going to be one of the greatest days of my life. To be so near the Queen was really something to me. The horses didn't interest me, although they were thoroughbreds. But who isn't? I always considered myself a thoroughbred. I am one of God's children, aren't we all?

The following day Jim came down all dressed up in top hat and all that went with it. He really made a big impression on me. I had a long dress and coat to match. It was a pretty shade of blue. I wore a large hat that was as pretty as a picture. My blonde hair was showing from under it. It gave me quite an attraction. Oh, yes, and I carried a parasol in a matching blue. I felt this was my day.

Jim had ordered a Bentley and a chauffeur to drive us to the races. I could see Jim gave me many glances of admiration. He remarked, "Darling, you look like a Queen. Here I was again, living the way I wanted to live. I kept telling myself I wished my father could see me now. I knew what he would say to me, "Good luck kiddo, you deserve it all."

We got to the races before it was time for the first race to start. Jim took me to the fabulous cocktail bar. It had everything, champagne flowing like water, caviar, and many different kinds of sandwiches. I'd have loved to have tried them all. I reminded myself to be a lady, two drinks and two sandwiches were the limit for me. Jim introduced me to a lot of nice people. He must be well known in these circles because it was always, "Hello Jim," or "Hello Jim darling," from the ladies. Then they would glance at me in wonderment. "Oh," Jim would say, "This is a very dear friend of mine. I want you to meet the future Mrs. Hatfield." I was astounded at this coming from Jim. I looked at him and he smiled sweetly at me. I couldn't remember Jim's last name. Was his surname Hatfield? No, I was sure not. But who was this Mr. Hatfield? I got to thinking Jim was playing a trick on me, maybe a joke. I held my tongue and returned the sweet smiles for all the people I met.

As we walked around the track, we talked about the horses and what chance they had to win. It kept coming back to me, who was this Mr. Hatfield? Who the heck could he be?

The first race was about to start. I picked a horse called, believe it or not, Molly Perkins. I most certainly was going to back it. I put one pound on it. I always made my bet for a win and place. It was 25 to 1, an outsider. I didn't think it had a chance of winning. Jim was on the favourite at 4 to 1.

We walked to the grandstand to watch the race. Seated two rows in front of where we were sitting was a beautiful lady and her escort. Yes, it was the Queen. No one seemed to rush to get near her. I guess these people were used to being so close to the Queen. I had never been so close to her. It was the greatest thrill for me.

The race got off to a good start. We all stood up to watch them run. Jim's horse was number five, mine was number seven, my lucky number. The favourite horse was winning, or I should say was leading by four lengths. That was Jim's horse. Mine was fourth, but was making a good pace. Then Molly took the lead. I was so excited. I kept on repeating, "Come on Molly, you can do it," And she did. Molly Perkins won by two lengths at 25 to 1, for me. The favourite was third, Jim had it backed for a place, so he won a little.

The next race they had a horse called Patsy. I, of course, backed it. There was a photo finish. I couldn't believe I could be lucky twice. but it showed on the photo that Patsy had won by a nose. Jim was laughing at my luck. I had never been so lucky, ever. It all seemed like a dream. I didn't want to wake up. Jim kept on meeting a lot of people he knew, and I was the main attraction to them. They couldn't guess who I was, and what Jim's intentions were towards me. The more I met these people, the more comfortable I felt being with them.

Most of the men looked military and retired, like Jim. One fellow
Jim introduced me to was an attractive man in his fifties. Jim told me
he was a bachelor and had never married. I wondered how a good
looker like him escaped it. The ladies must have all been slow takers. I
didn't catch his surname, but heard he was called Jerry. That suited
him so well. He was quite a charmer.

Jerry would leave us then come back several times. We just
couldn't get rid of him. He would come back just to tell us he hadn't
backed one single winner. He asked me to pick one in the next two
races. I did this for him, one won and the other came second. So he did
win some money. By now he wouldn't leave us. I was enjoying his
company. Jim could see that.

Jim had known Jerry for many years. He knew Jerry was a real
ladies man. The women just fell for him all the time. I thought I'd
better go slow with this fellow because he seemed so sure of himself.
Not conceited, but self assured. I like people like that. They do
something for me.

We got home safe and sound after a beautiful day. The sun had
come out and everywhere you looked there were the beautiful women
and men I had once dreamed of. Jim's leg was tiring a little, he wanted
to lie down. "Good night dear. Sleep well," he said. I rushed up to kiss
him and thank him for such a wonderful day.

I kissed him on the cheek and said, "Thank you Mr. Hatfield."
He just laughed and turned, going up to his flat. I got to thinking again
about this Mr. Hatfield. I was sure that wasn't Jerry's surname,
although I didn't catch it when Jim introduced me. I kept thinking,
who it could be whose wife I was supposed to become later? I couldn't
sleep all night wondering who this character was. I thought I wouldn't
pressure Jim into telling me who it was. It would come out later, I
presumed. Maybe it's best forgotten. It could just be one of Jim's jokes
with his friends.

I kept thinking about Jim. He had a very appealing manner,
something that every woman liked. Maybe he had something hidden
that a woman would enjoy. I felt I'd have to be patient with him. I'd
have to know for a long time before I could really understand his way
of thinking.

Jim came down next day to have his usual four o'clock cuppa
with me. We had just sat down to enjoy our tea when the doorbell
rang. I almost always answered the door to save Jim walking down.
When I opened the door, I saw a tall fellow whom I recognised from

being at the races the day before. Yes, it was Jerry. "Is Jim in?" He enquired

"Oh, yes. Come on in," I said with caution, he seemed to be the pushy type of person. Jim seemed glad to see him, as they had known each other for many years. We sat talking in my front sitting room. Jim kept referring to him as Jerry. Now, what was his surname? I was anxiously waiting to hear it. I had met so many people at the races, I couldn't remember all their surnames.

Jerry stayed so long, Jim invited him to stay for a meal with him upstairs. When Jerry finally left, Jim told me that Jerry was a real lady killer. All the ladies would fall for him, but he had never married. Jim said he was too smart for that. Jerry was financially independent. He was the only child of wealthy parents, lived at the coast, and had a housekeeper living with him. It was funny Jim didn't tell me that Jerry was living in one of Molly's houses that now belonged to me. I didn't think Jerry knew this. I didn't know the names of my tenants as my solicitor was looking after all my affairs. Jim thought I would know all about my affairs.

I started to wonder if Jerry could be this Mr. Hatfield, the lady killer. His friends evidently thought that some day there would be a Mrs. Hatfield, and I guess they thought it could be me. I now more sure than ever that he was Mr. Hatfield.

I talked to Jim for quite a while after Jerry had gone. I asked him outright if I was right in thinking that Jerry was Mr. Hatfield, and what was the joke when he introduced me as the future Mrs. Hatfield. "Darling, you are so right. He is Mr. Hatfield, and I knew only too well when he met you, he would propose marriage. He is chasing you."

"Oh Jim, I don't think that could happen to me." It seems all Jerry's friends knew he would chase a newcomer to the party. Well, that settled that. I knew Mr. Hatfield, and he was a charmer, but he didn't appeal to me one little bit. I thought he was a conceited man who needed to be slapped down and I was the one to do it if I wished to. Maybe he was a show-off and his true nature was different. I hoped so as there was something about Jerry that appealed to me.

Jim didn't know I had a married son, as I hadn't heard from him for a long time. He wrote once to say he had two children and a very prosperous business. I guess he was too busy to write to me more often, and I hadn't written to tell him of my good fortune. I wasn't worried about him, I knew they were all happy.

Jerry would phone me every day to have a little chat about nothing. He did ask me many times to visit him. I thought that was a good idea to see my property, my three houses were close together. I called Jerry and he met me at the station and drove me to his house. I didn't tell Jim about this as I knew he wouldn't be pleased at all.

I was greatly impressed with Jerry's house. It was in good condition for an older house. He had looked after it inside and outside. Jerry gave me a tour through his home. I must admit it was beautiful, mostly all modern and expensive.

We sat and drank our tea in his lounge that overlooked the ocean. He really disturbed my thoughts when he said, "You know, Martha, the first time I set eyes on you I knew you were made for me." I looked him straight in the eye and asked how he knew my name was Martha. It seems Molly used to talk to him about me and how kind I was to her. So that solved the mystery.

"Jerry please don't call me Martha, I don't like it."

But he said, "Martha was my mother's name and I love it."

I got used to it. He just loved to call me Martha. I kind of liked it as I grew to understand Jerry. He was a different man to what I had thought. He was a member of two private clubs in London. You had to be someone special to become a member. I got so involved with Jerry, Jim kept warning me about his past love affairs that came to nothing. I was not concerned at all. Jerry was good fun and he did something for me mentally. I kept telling Jim, "I am not in love with Jerry. I am just having fun with him. I am not dumb. I know why the chicken crossed the road, and I realise also my reputation could be in danger of criticism. Jim darling, why should I care what people think about me?" I think Jim was missing me since Jerry took over.

Jerry owned about five greyhound racing dogs. He took me to see them run. I always loved dogs. Any make would appeal to me. I really fell for these dogs and I bought two. I called them Martha and Molly. Sad to say they never won one race. Jerry was a big gambler. As the time went by, I also became a big gambler. I lost a lot of money. That caused me to have to sell the house I was living in. It was too big for me anyway. Jim was very upset when I told him I was selling Molly's house. He didn't want to leave there, or lose me.

I had sold it and my solicitor informed me that one of my houses at the coast was coming vacant. I was happy about that. It answered my problem. I could live in it. This was a ten bed roomed house overlooking the ocean. It wasn't far from where I managed the apartment house some years previously.

I had the house converted into two flats, each having its own entrance. I had it painted inside and out. It looked lovely. I asked Jim if he wanted the upstairs flat, but he wouldn't leave Molly's house. I didn't dare ask Jerry, as he would be there before I moved in. He lived just a block away from there.

I moved into this beautiful flat. I had to sell many of Molly's things and I bought new modern furniture. I was really enjoying the ocean view. I rented the upstairs flat to a nice couple called Hanson. They were a retired, lovable husband and wife. To me they looked too young to retire. I found out later they owned a pub in town and had a manager running it for them. When I heard this I was back to where I had started. I got the urge to return to the bar work. I wanted to get back into the swing of things as I loved meeting people. Jerry was still around but we had sold our racing dogs at a big loss. I promised myself to stay off gambling altogether.

There was going to be a big party at one of Jerry's clubs in town and he insisted I should go with him. He wouldn't take no for an answer from me. I got to thinking, how many ladies had he taken to these clubs? Why should I worry? There's no harm in me going. I knew I would love meeting Jerry's friends.

We arrived at six. I was surprised to see what a fabulous place it was. It had everything one could wish for, a maid showed us to the cloakroom that was up a flight of winding stairs carpeted with a bright red carpet, and all over the upstairs. It was beautiful. I didn't know one could stay over night, or for a long weekend. We had a lovely dinner with wine. Also champagne and cocktails were there for one to enjoy. Between dances we would visit the bar. Jerry excused himself to go to the men's room, so I thought. He seemed to be longer than necessary. I sat there waiting for him to return, just relaxing with my legs sprawled out. A gentleman who looked to be in his fifties was passing me, tripped over one of my feet, and fell flat on his face. That really shook me up too. I apologised and helped him up. He said, "Please don't apologise, it was my fault for not looking where I was going." He immediately asked me for a dance. I accepted as Jerry hadn't returned yet. He was a very attractive sort of fellow.

After the dance, we sat on the other side of the room. We had a very interesting talk, and he suggested we should meet again. He handed me his card and said, "Phone me one day when you feel in the mood." I couldn't think of what kind of mood he would expect me to be in to phone him. It left me guessing.

Where was Jerry all this time? I walked across the room hoping to see him. There he was with a waiter who was pushing a trolley on wheels. It had a large cake on it with a big sign. As I walked towards Jerry, he shouted, "Martha, where have you been?" The nearer I got to the cake, I could read the sign. It read, 'Welcome Martha, to the lovers Club.' They all stood around the cake and clapped. That was a big surprise for me. What was I supposed to do next? I must make a thank you speech. At that time I was feeling very exuberant, and the champagne certainly helped. I made a very brief thank you to all concerned and everyone enjoyed the cake and ice cream.

That was about nine o'clock. The night was young yet. Jerry and I danced till 11;30. We both were feeling a little exhausted from all the excitement. Jerry said he had gone to the front entrance to the club and saw a blanket of thick fog. "Darling, we can't drive home in this fog. We shall have to stay the night." I said to myself, should we? I guess I'll have to agree to it. I don't like foggy nights of any description.

I learned later that Jerry had already booked a double room when we arrived at the club. I didn't really object to that arrangement, but I think Jerry could have warned me that this would happen. I hadn't anything to wear in the sleeping line, nor had Jerry, I presumed.

When we retired to our room, I was surprised to see a king sized bed, and mirrors on the ceiling. That puzzled me. What were mirrors doing up there? I found out as the evening grew. Thrown on the bed were a pair of beautiful silk men's pyjamas, and a flimsy topless nightgown for me. I thought, all this and heaven too? As the cocktails were still with me, I didn't think anything could matter now..

The chambermaid came to ask if there was anything she could do for the lady. Now, what else did I need? The only thing I could think of was that brick my mother had told me to keep both feet on, to be safe. I didn't think I would have any trouble with Jerry. He was a blow bag at times and blow bags sometimes burst in mid air.

Jerry went for a shower. The perfume coming from the bathroom was very tantalising for me. I also took a shower. Afterwards we lay on the bed talking for an hour. Well, it seemed like an hour to me, things were not happening as I expected they would. Jerry was supposed to be a lady killer and could manage them all. It came to my mind several times as we lay there, what were we waiting for? The buses don't pass here anyway. My love life had been sadly neglected for six years now. It wasn't for me to take the first move, so we kept on talking.

Jerry had many things to tell me about his past life. Somehow I must have encouraged him to tell me. Being a good listener, he appreciated it.

It had got to 1:30. Jerry rang a bell for a pot of tea to be brought to our room. I thought that was a nice idea. It would break the monotony we were both experiencing. When the maid arrived with the tea, she inquired to Jerry, "Is everything all right, sir?"

"Oh yes, just fine, thank you."

We enjoyed our tea and again relaxed on the bed. Was this the romance I had once dreamed of? I was feeling sorry for myself now. We just didn't get around to expressing our feelings for each other. To me this was an unusual affair. It was 2:30. I was nearly going to sleep. Jerry suddenly started to make a confession to me. He seemed to go out of his way to explain his situation. I just couldn't think of anything at this time of the morning. "Jerry, why don't we go to sleep and you tell me in the morning?"

"All right darling, if you wish." I was asleep within minutes with Jerry's arms around me.

I woke up about seven. Jerry had been up and showered and had ordered tea for us. We both dressed and had tea near the window. I was still pondering what Jerry had to tell me. It couldn't be about all the ladies he had loved. He wouldn't confess anything like that to me. I wasn't interested in his previous love affairs. I was mostly interested in our precious night we had together. What was his problem? Jerry was a very lovable man. I just couldn't understand him. I came to the conclusion he was incapable of sex.

At last he began to tell me his problem. Jerry caught polio 10 years ago and it had left him immune from all sexual acts. It was quite a blow to me. I expressed my sorrow to Jerry, but I assured him I still loved him in a different way.

That evening I thought he was just being a gentleman to me. But I have never met one like him to confess his failure of his manhood on an evening shared together. It must be a great let-down for him to take. He was always a very generous man to his loves. I had decided to accept him as he was.

After we had breakfast, Jerry suggested we would do some shopping. We looked through several jewellery shops. Jerry knew I was fond of nice jewellery. He wanted to buy me something in remembrance of the night we had spent together. We looked at rings, bracelets. I always liked pearls, I mean real pearls. Jerry bought me two strands of beautiful perfect pearls. I was overwhelmed by his generosity and I thanked him a million. I felt I didn't earn all this generosity, but he insisted he had a wonderful evening and loved every minute of it.

I didn't see Jerry for nearly a week. He did phone me every day as usual to tell me how much he loved me and hoped one day I would become the first Mrs. J. Hatfield. He seemed convinced I would marry him one day. Right now, much as I loved Jerry, I didn't know if it would be wise to take on a marriage like this. I knew it would be all the love and no sex life. I had experienced this kind of marriage once before. I couldn't possibly go through it again. I felt like the Irishman who fell from a 20 story building and lost his way down. It would take time for both of us to realise that kind of marriage wouldn't work.

I got a call from Jim. He said he had been sick and would I go to see him as he missed me so much. I felt I really didn't want to start up another close relationship with Jim again. He wasn't my kind after all. So I made an excuse to the fact that I was working again and I had not the time to visit him just then.

Mr. and Mrs. Hanson, who lived upstairs, would come down to visit me. They realised I lived alone and would appreciate their company. They told me they were having trouble getting the right type of manager in the pub they owned and asked me if I would be interested in co-management of their pub. Wow! What an offer to me! I told them previously I had many years experience in the pubs and hotel work. I said I would think about it. I'd loved to have accepted the offer right away, but I didn't want to appear too keen for the job.

I told Jerry about this offer. He was upset at the very thought of Martha working in a pub, and of course he was hoping I would become his wife before long. I thought about this very seriously. That was the life I was happy to be amongst. Jerry was putting me under an obligation to him. Now, I thought, how can I please Jerry and please myself? I didn't see why Jerry should be so demanding.

I talked to Jim about it and he agreed with me to take the job. "If it will make you happy, I say go to it."

Jim helped me to decide. I went upstairs to talk to Mrs. Hanson about their offer of co-managing their pub. She was delighted. I had accepted the job. It was just part time. They wanted me there in the evenings. That suited me fine. I loved the company. My hours would be 6:00 until midnight. I would be responsible for the cash. "Pat, you can start just as soon as you are ready." I suggested Saturday. "That's fine. I'll see you then and introduce you to the manager."

The manager was French. He was very nice and spoke good English, so that was no problem. My first night was Saturday. It's always a busy night with weekenders coming in, quite a good class of people. These were the people I enjoyed. I seemed to be living in a different atmosphere now.

The weeks went by so fast; they do when one is happy and content, having met some nice men. One gentleman owned a massage parlour and a keep fit class. That interested me very much. I needed to lose about 10 pounds that I had put on the last few weeks. Caviar and cocktails aren't good for me. I told him I wanted to get back to my normal weight. He immediately invited me down to his parlour. I enquired about the charges, but he said, "Don't worry about that, Pat. I want you to see how we can make you lose 10 to 15 pounds within a few days."

I made an appointment. I was surprised to see so many people who looked in their fifties and some older. I really enjoyed this treatment. It made me feel so much younger. I thought about Joe who used to tickle the old lady's feet to relax her. That could have been the start of a massage parlour for Joe, had he kept up his tickling to all parts of the body. Joe could have been a wealthy man now.

I was very pleased that I had lost 15 pounds and felt and looked so much younger. My figure was more in shape too. I seemed to be getting more attention now, mostly from men in particular.

I had many invitations to go to the theatres. I loved ballet and knew one day I would accept this invitation.

I had a strange encounter with one of our gentlemen customers. He just looked at me and smiled, and said, "Do you remember me Pat?"

I looked at him again and I knew he was the fellow who had fallen over my feet at the Lover's Club some weeks before. He had given me his card but I must have lost it. I could see her was surprised to see me working in a pub, but he was very sweet to me and asked me when I was free to make a date with him. I thought he was rushing things. I told him I was too busy to make arrangements. That seemed to settle him for a while. He came in to see me most every night. I got

to know him as Ron. I didn't know his full name. He remarked he
saw me dancing with Jerry often. I said, "Yes, he is a very dear friend
of mine."

"How long have you known Jerry?"

"Oh, quite a while," I replied with an enquiring look.

"You know Jerry is a well known lady killer. I see he didn't
succeed in marrying you."

"No, I am not ready for marriage yet. I am still waiting for Mr.
Right." He repeated what I had just said. He also was waiting for Miss
Right. Who's he kidding? He must be in his fifties, or near it. He still
was a very charming man.

Ron came in as usual every night. I also got an unexpected
visit from Jerry. I didn't know these two men knew each other. I think
they surprised each other. As they met they shook hands and had a
drink together. I noticed Jerry kept a close eye on Ron. He seemed to
be resenting Ron's familiarity with me. Jerry made sure he was going
to escort me home after the pub had closed.

On the way home Jerry started to ask questions about Ron.
How did I know him? When I told him the truth, he seemed to doubt
my story. I had to convince him many times before he knew I was
telling him the truth. After a little more talking about Ron, I realised
why Jerry should doubt my story. Ron had told him I had made a date
with him to take me to the theatre the next week. Men are so childish
at times. Why did he have to tell Jerry, even if it was true? Jerry told
me Ron had been married and divorced twice. That was a different
story than Ron had told me. I think Jerry still had hopes I would marry
him. I knew in my heart I couldn't take on another marriage like that,
as sweet as he was to me. Nature demands more than Jerry could give
me.

I still hadn't got a bill from Tom for my six visits to his
massage parlour. I had asked him many times for my bill but he just
ignored it. He got me thinking how I could repay his generosity. I soon
found out. Within a couple of weeks he was knocking on my front
door. I was really shocked when I opened the door to see Tom
standing there with a huge bunch of red roses. These were my
favourite flowers. What else could I say but, "Come on in and I will
make you a cup of tea." I repeated my request for my bill from Tom.

"Darling, please don't mention that bill again. It was my
pleasure."

What else could I say but, "Thank you Tom," and I gave him a peck on his cheek. That was the beginning of a serious love affair between us. Tom had been divorced from his first wife three years before and he said he had never met anyone since who he loved and wanted to marry until he met me just a few weeks ago. We seemed to be growing closer every day. Jerry knew this but kept quiet; he never asked me how this could happen to me so suddenly.

I knew Tom pretty well now. He had told me most of his past life. One thing that he didn't tell me was that he had five children. Oh heck, that was a shocker. Jerry didn't tell me this. I heard it from one of the customers who knew Tom. He thought I knew he had children. My, oh my! The thought of taking on the job to bring up five children! The eldest was 16. I just couldn't tolerate the idea of marrying Tom now, that was unreasonable for him to ask me to marry him. I tried to cool our relations slowly because I didn't want to hurt his feelings. I would go out with Jerry occasionally. I thought it would change the picture a little.

I don't know why Tom didn't tell me about his family. I presume he thought I wouldn't accept his proposal of marriage if I knew he had five children. However, he was financially stable; he had several parlours under management.

However weeks went by and Tom was beginning to console himself. He must have thought I wouldn't make a good step mother to five children. I was very disappointed in Tom. He was a little younger than I, but that wasn't the problem between us. I couldn't see why he had not married before this as he was a very prosperous business man, and could give a wife all she needed. I guess it must have been his family that was the drawback. That would be a big responsibility for someone.

He told me his wife was an alcoholic. That caused him to divorce her. I was sorry for him, but I didn't change my decision not to marry him.

Chapter Six.

Well, back to Jerry again. He was always a good standby for me, and I had a soft spot in my heart for him. He agreed with my decision regards Tom's proposal of marriage. I think Jerry was happy about that. I was beginning to think that way myself, although I thought I loved Tom, but not his five children.

I hadn't seen Jim for several weeks. I had heard he was moving to the coast. It seemed he wanted to be nearer to me, and I wanted him to come here. He was a grand fellow.

Christmas was coming up soon. That's the time everyone gets happy. There were lots of parties. Christmas for me had not been a happy time over the past years. I was always alone. I had a feeling this Christmas was going to be different. I loved my job in the pub. I got on well with the manager, R. Chaval. We called him Jean. He was a very conscientious worker. Everyone was fond of him and I got on well with him.

On Christmas Eve Jean and I were invited to a private party. I didn't know Jean's wife was an invalid. She had had a stroke just two years before. It had left her a very sick person. They had one son who lived away somewhere. I had never heard who these people were who had invited Jean and me to this private party. They said Jean could bring a friend, so he asked me to go along with him. It was being held at one of the private clubs not far from the pub. I told Jerry about it and he wasn't too pleased that I should go unless I took him. Jean suggested otherwise. We would go together without Jerry. So I agreed to that.

After the pub closed, Jean and I took a cab to the party. When we arrived it was in full swing. Everyone was happy and full of champagne, cocktails, etc. Jean knew many of the people and introduced me to a number of men friends of his. I danced with quite a few. I lost sight of Jean altogether. I didn't see him until the party was coming to a close. It was past midnight then. I got worried about Jean. What had happened to him? A gentleman came to tell me he had been called to the hospital. His son had been in a car accident. That was why I couldn't find him.

Jean returned to the club later to take me home. We all were anxious to know how his son was. At the time he was in a coma. It looked as if Jean was going to have another sick person to look after. This wasn't a very happy party.

Jean dropped me home, and I thanked him for what could have been a happy party. I had many invitations during the evening, but I thought it wouldn't be nice of me to accept them. Christmas day was a quiet day, good to relax after an unexpected sad evening for us all.

I got a phone call from Jim. He had moved into a nice apartment close by me. He asked me to go round to see it. When I arrived, the kettle was boiling for a nice cuppa. He was so sweet to me. I gave him an extra look. I could see he had something to tell me. I noticed his eyes looked dull. He wasn't his usual self. I asked him, "Are you all right Jim?"

He replied with caution, "No Pat, I had tests and they tell me I have cancer of the liver and I have only three months to live."

"Oh, Jim, my love, I don't believe it. This can't be true." But it was.

Jerry and I tried to make him as happy as possible under such awful circumstances. We planned a New Years party for Jim just for a few people at my flat. We invited some people whom Jim was fond of. Jerry came and it was a lovely evening. Jim enjoyed his dear friends, but I couldn't let myself go. I kept thinking of Jim. I shall miss him. I couldn't bear the thought of losing him. Jim had no living relations, he was the only child. He once told me he had one son, but he didn't accept Jim as his father. It seems he lived with his mother and never came to see Jim

The weeks just dragged on. Jim became a very sick man. He had a nurse with him around the clock. Jim only lasted six weeks. I was glad he didn't suffer too long. I wondered who was going to settle his estate. Jerry was involved in most of his assets. When Jim's will was published, Jerry had been given all Jim's antiques. They were very valuable. Jim had shares in many different companies. He left quite a bit to charity. I was surprised to hear he had left me his grand piano that I had always admired.

Jerry was very upset at losing a lifelong friend like Jim. He seemed to come and visit me more since Jim passed on. Jerry had changed considerably in the past months. I begged of him to stop worrying about Jim. "Jim is at peace now. So you must step out of all this gloomy state." It was hard for me to tell Jerry this as I was feeling pretty down myself. I missed Jim phoning me every day. I told Jerry, "I think we both need a holiday." He could see I wasn't the same Pat.

Jerry suggested we take a cruise to relax. I never had a longing to go anywhere else but the U.S.A., my country where I was born. I thought, shall we go to the U.S.A?

Jerry was very persistent, "Why don't we go, Pat?" It didn't take me long to decide on going. So I packed up the job at the pub as I didn't seem to be getting anywhere with it. Mrs. Hanson was very disappointed that I was leaving their pub, but I told her that something had to happen to me soon. I couldn't take this depression. Jerry was thrilled with the idea that we should go to the place where I was born. Jerry thought we should fly; but no, I said I wanted to relax on a boat for a few days.

Jerry booked our fare on the Queen Mary. I was so pleased about that. We had just three weeks to prepare for the trip. I was beginning to feel alive again. I had no time now to entertain anyone. Mrs. Hanson, we called her Meg, came down to have a cup of tea with me and the usual bits of scandal we enjoyed now and then. What she told me was quite a big bit of scandal I had never heard before. She told me Jim had lived with a woman for five years and she turned up to claim some part of his fortune. Jim gave her some shares many years ago when they were living together. What a surprise to me. I had never connected any woman in Jim's life. He always seemed a loner. I guess I judged wrong.

I was looking forward to our trip to the U.S.A. I got a kind of guilty feeling. Why am I taking this trip? Does it mean so much to me? Sometimes my mother's sayings used to come back to my mind, 'Happiness is where it is found and seldom where it is sought'.

Well, Jerry had booked it now, so I'd have to go and hope I'd enjoy it.

The Queen Mary was a beautiful boat. The meals were fabulous and there was lots of fun and games. Jerry kept a close eye on me most of the time until we docked in New York.

I had met several nice people on board. We had a few happy hours, but Jerry wasn't too far away. I kept wishing I had not accepted Jerry's company on this trip, but he had paid for it so I had to be nice to him.

We met an English gentleman who said this was his twenty sixth crossing, four times on the Queen Mary. He seemed to know the Captain and his crew. He was a man well preserved in his fifties. He looked the type who had led a clean life, but who knows? He always sat at the Captains table. He was introduced to us as Mr. William Worth. It sounded good to me. We called him Bill.

There was a party given at the Captains table for a few chosen guests. Jerry and I were invited. This was the night before we docked. It was a fabulous party. Everyone had gifts placed beside their plates. I noticed mine looked very special. I waited for everyone to open their gift before I started to open mine. I was feeling kind of guilty for some reason. Bill sat opposite to us. He gave me the sweetest smile. I was anxious to know what this gift could be to me from Bill. I opened it very slowly, as Jerry's eyes were popping out just longing to see what the gift was. Well, it revealed a great surprise for me. It was a beautiful gold evening purse. I looked across at Bill and gave him my sweetest smile and said, "Thank you, dear." Jerry didn't like this one little bit.

Just before we docked Bill came to me and invited me to call him whilst I was in New York. He repeated, "Don't worry about accommodation. I have plenty of rooms and you can stay as long as you wish." He gave me his phone number. Bill told me he had 10 apartments in the Bronx.

As we left the boat, Bill waved and said, "I'll see you soon." How soon, I thought? He was a very fascinating fellow; I'd love to meet him again, but it didn't seem possible with Jerry around.

Jerry and I had a wonderful three weeks. We were on the go all the time, dinners, theatres, etc. We went to see the town where I was born. It was not how I remembered it to be. We walked a lot round New York. At night we were ready to retire at nine o'clock. These three weeks went by so quickly. I was hoping we would see Bill again, but I didn't know how that could be arranged as Jerry wasn't interested in seeing him again. I believe he was jealous of Bill.

The last night in New York became a nightmare to me. Jerry was helping me pack up when he collapsed on the floor next to my luggage. I was shocked. I tried to revive him, but he was really out for the count. I called the desk operator and asked for a doctor as quickly as possible. I kept looking at Jerry. He didn't seem to be breathing. The doctor arrived and Jerry was taken to the nearest hospital. I went along with him and stayed at the hospital all evening. Jerry was in a coma. He didn't even know me. I was in a terrible state of mind as we were supposed to sail back to England the next day. The doctor said no way could Jerry be moved.

So I cancelled the voyage back on the Queen Mary. I stayed on at the same hotel. Three days had passed and Jerry was still in a coma. I was getting very anxious. I just did not know what to do. I knew I must stay with Jerry until he was better. It could be weeks.

I suddenly thought about Bill. I looked up his phone number and I plucked up courage and phoned him. A ladies voice came on to answer the phone. Who was she I thought? He told me he had never been married. I guessed it was his housekeeper. Bill was out just then and she said he would call me back later. I gave her the hospital number also our hotel number.

It was so late that I went to bed. At mid night the call came through. Bill couldn't believe it could be me calling him as we were supposed to be on the Queen Mary on our way back home. "Hello Bill. This is Pat." What a shock he got. He was so excited to hear my voice he nearly came through the wires to me.

"Where are you darling? I thought you were back in England now." Before I had finished telling him the sad story about Jerry, he shouted, "Don't worry dear, I'll be right over." I told him the hotel. It seems he knew it well. He had no problem to find me. When I saw Bill again, I was nearly ashamed to say I had fallen for him. He seemed to be the man I always wanted.

Bill took me to the hospital several times. There was no change in Jerry's condition. I asked the doctor how long he expected Jerry to be in this coma. He told me he could not predict any time, as he could die any time or could live for a few months. Bill begged of me to live in with him. He helped me to pack all my clothes also Jerry's belongings. We had quite a car load. When we arrived at Bill's apartments I got a surprise to see he lives in a very nice neighbourhood. His apartments looked new. I always thought the Bronx was not a nice area to live in. I imagined it would be amongst the down-towners, all kinds of people.

As we entered the ground floor apartment an elderly grey haired lady greeted us. Bill introduced me to her as his housekeeper. That came as a relief to me. I had formed the idea when I heard a ladies voice on the phone that it might be Bill's wife or lady love. I was so happy about this.

She showed me to my room and brought me a cup of tea, which I needed so badly. Bill took our luggage into another room as there was so much of Jerry's things. I kept thinking about Jerry. What would he think of all this? Bill was so kind to me I don't know what I would have done without him.

It was four weeks now since Jerry fell sick. I kept asking, "Should I go home to England?"

When I mentioned this to Bill, he wouldn't hear of it. "You must stay here as long as Jerry is here."

Up to now Bill had been a perfect gentleman in every way to me. I was beginning to like him in a brotherly way, if there was such a thing as brotherly love. Time was going fast. I was just wishing Jerry would come out of that coma, when the phone rang. It was from the hospital to say Jerry had passed on just a half hour before. Oh, dear God, I couldn't believe it. What could I do now? I knew Jerry had a sister in England somewhere, but where? Bill helped me.

I had Jerry's body flown back to England for burial. I contacted Jerry's solicitor. He looked after everything. I wanted to fly back to England for Jerry's funeral but Bill didn't like the idea of me flying back alone. "I'll go with you love," he remarked. How could I refuse?

We arrived just in time for the burial the following day. Bill was pleased he could do all this for me. He seemed to like staying at my apartment, and there was no mention when he would return to the Bronx. I didn't encourage him either way.

The people in the upstairs apartment got to know Bill and enjoyed his company. It was two weeks now since we had arrived back in England. We were having breakfast together one morning and Bill gave me a sharp glance and smiled at me. "What's on your mind Bill?" I thought, what could be next?

He reached over to touch my hand, "Darling, I love you more than you think. Please forgive me saying this, but I feel I just can't live without having you around me."

What could I say, but, "Bill, I am very fond of you and I appreciate your kindness. I don't understand your feelings towards me. Is this a proposal of marriage Bill?" "Yes. Yes it is, darling."

I was in a confused state of mind right now. "Bill, I can't answer that just now." It seemed he had made up his mind to marry me. I didn't thing he was a quick worker on love making. We hadn't got to that stage yet. I just passed it off and said we would talk about that another day.

Jerry was often on my mind, although I didn't love him. He was always there when I needed him. Bill's proposal was too swift for me to take. I kept thinking about him. He told me he was a bachelor.

I was on my way to my room when I met Bess, Bill's housekeeper. She came into my room. We both sat on the edge of my bed. We started to talk about Bill. She told me he was the son of a Baptist Minister and she had been his housekeeper for 15 years. I thought that solved a lot of my previous doubts about Bill. I must talk to him about his past life, had he married? Has he any family?

As Bess was leaving the room she ran into Bill. He was coming to have a talk with me. Before he could talk, I said, "Bill, I have many things to ask you. Sit down. I want you to answer a few questions."

He looked surprised at my request, looked at me and said. "Darling, what do you want to now about me? I am just another human being. My father was a Baptist Minister. I am 55 years young. I am in good health and of sound mind. I have never been married, but I love to travel the world, and I do admire pretty women like you, Pat. Is there anything wrong with that?"

"No," I replied, "I guess not. But Bill, I haven't known you for a very long time. I feel I'd like a little more time before I can say yes or no. I don't want to lose you. Please be patient with me."

Many weeks had passed and Bill was still here. He decided it was time he left for the Bronx. When I said goodbye at the airport, he looked really sad. I felt the same way. I didn't know how long I could live here without Bill and Jerry. I missed them both. When that plane left the ground I wept. When I was going to see Bill again?

I got a phone call from Bill every week, sometimes twice a week. He was still hoping I would return to the Bronx and marry him. As the weeks went by I seemed to be getting a closer feeling to Bill. I was desperately lonely.

One night I got a phone call from Jean, who used to manage the pub. He was in a pretty low state. I begged of him to tell me what was the problem. I asked him to come round and have a talk with me. "You will feel better, Jean. I will help you if it's possible."

He was around very soon knocking on my door. "Come on in Jean. What can I do for you? I'll make you a cup of tea." We talked for two hours. It seemed longer than that. I was very upset when he told me his wife had taken an overdose of her medicine and had died the night before. I t was a blessing in disguise as she had suffered for many years. I knew his son had a car accident months ago. He was still in a wheelchair, unable to walk.

Well, he sure had troubles. "Pat," He asked, "Would you come to me house and help me for a few days?" What else could I say, but yes.

I stayed until after the funeral of his wife. He thanked me many times. It helped me to help him. My problems seemed so small now.

Months passed and Jean would visit me at least once a week. He had left the management of Mrs. Hanson's pub and was working for a big whiskey firm in London, requiring him to travel.

One day he phoned me to ask if I'd like to go up to London. He had a few calls to make. "Maybe you would like to do some shopping." I accepted right away. I needed this.

We had a great day. Jean introduced me to a few of his clients who were in the whiskey business. We had dinner at one of the finest hotels. I was grateful to Jean for thinking of me. I thanked him and he gave me a little hug and said, "Good night, Pat. I love you for the help you have given me." He didn't know how much I needed this day out with him.

Chapter Seven.

When I got home I had lots of mail waiting for me. One letter was from Jerry's solicitor asking me to make an appointment to see him soon. I phoned him and saw him the following morning. I wondered why he wanted to see me, maybe because I still had Jerry's belongings, his watch and diamond ring he took on the trip. I wanted to get rid of them but I didn't know how. I had no idea of Jerry's wealth. I did hear he was a wealthy man. The way he lived it was obvious. Jerry was my tenant and he had an apartment full of beautiful furniture, etc., that must have been valuable. I couldn't touch anything until the will was passed.

I understood the solicitor to say I was the intended Mrs. Hatfield soon. I didn't deny that, because Jerry had always wanted me to become Mrs. Hatfield. "Mrs. Armstrong, Jerry has been very generous to you in his will." This was a big surprise for me. Jerry had left me all his personal belongings, his car and an income for life of £10.000 a year. I couldn't believe it. He also had left a lot to different charities, to animals and to an old people's home. Ten thousand a year! What could I do with all that money? Maybe I'd need it one day when I would be old and couldn't work. Thank you Jerry darling.

I didn't tell a soul about my good fortune, or maybe I'd be getting some proposals of marriage. I still heard from Bill every week. I loved to hear his voice. I was still getting over the shock of Jerry's ten thousand a year income.

The summer was here and all the schools were on vacation. I thought I'd write my son and invite the family down. They could stay in Jerry's house. They were pleased to come and arrived two days later. I hadn't seen the children since they were babies. Now they were 8 and 10 years old. They were well behaved children. I just loved them. David, my son, was a very strict father and his wife Pamela was very devoted to her family. We had fun together for six weeks. I gave David Jerry's gold watch and cigarette case and his diamond ring and some antiques I didn't want. Before they left I gave them all a big sum of money to put into their bank account. I felt I didn't need all that money as Molly had left me comfortable too. I enjoyed them, but I missed them now that I was alone again.

Jerry's house was too big for me so I had it made into two apartments with separate entrances. I rented them to two professional men. One was a doctor and the other a solicitor. They seemed to fit well together. The doctor, Mr. Johnson, was on the ground floor and Mr. Blair was upstairs. I got to know them as Al and Pete. They were very friendly people. There didn't seem to be any problems.

I got so lonely at times I used to go and help them out at the pub where I used to work. There was a new manager now. He looked to be in his sixties, a very charming man, just the type they needed in a pub. I could see he was very popular. He and I got on fine together. As weeks went by he asked me if I would work more hours. I started to work four nights a week, I was loving it again. I surely didn't need the money; it was the company of these people I needed so badly. I had lost Jim and Jerry. I had Bill but he was too far away from me, although he was there when I needed him. I was always sure of his help any time. I knew it meant marriage for Bill. That I didn't want yet. With all the wealth I had now I thought it had spoiled me and made me feel independent from anyone. Again, I remembered my father's sayings, 'Happiness consists of the fewness of your wants.' I guess he was right.

On the way home from the pub one evening I was walking along the promenade. It was a beautiful evening. I came across a crowd of people. As I was passing, I noticed a dog lying down. I went up to them to ask if I could help. What was wrong with the dog? I am very fond of dogs. They told me he was hit by a passing car. His leg was broken. One of the men went for his car that was parked nearby and took the dog to a vet. I wondered who he was. That was the only bit of excitement I had that night.

Several weeks later that gentleman who looked after the dog came into the pub. I was so pleased to see him again to ask about the dog. He said the dog was fine now. "He was a lost dog so I gave him a home. I live alone so he is good company for me. Why don't you come round and see Rip? He is a lovely dog."

He gave me his card and I thanked him for being so kind to Rip, "I will come and see him one of these days."

We were very busy in the pub that night and I didn't get much time to tal to him. Fred, the manager, said to me after the pub was closed, I didn't know you knew Mr. Hall."

"I don't really," I said, and told him how I met him. Fred went on to tell me that this Mr. Hall was a highly respected gentleman in this town. He did a lot of charity work. He was a retired young fellow in his fifties.

Mr. Hall made a habit of calling at the pub most evenings. He became very friendly with me and asked me, "Why don't you come round and see Rip tomorrow afternoon?"

I replied, "OK, I'll be there about three o'clock."

He would insist on picking me up in his car. When it arrived it was a new Bentley. That was quite a car. Mr. Hall was a real gentleman, but he did say for me to call him Ed, short for Edward.

We had a happy meeting with Rip. He was a coon breed, but so lovable. He wasn't too big, just the right size for a house dog. Rip had his own bedroom. I was surprised to see the size of Ed's apartment. Ed gave me a tour of his place, beautifully furnished. There were six rooms and two bathrooms. All seemed very modern. That was a change for me to see modern furniture instead of old antique stuff. I always preferred the modern touch in all things.

I saw quite a bit of Ed. He would be in the pub most nights. I got to looking forward to seeing him. I never took my car to work as the pub was just walking distance from my apartment. I liked to walk. Ed got the idea I would prefer to ride home, so he would insist on driving me home. He would come in for a cuppa and stay for an hour. I really got to enjoy his company. Time had passed so quickly since I met Ed. I had known him three months now. He wasn't the pushy type.

One evening he asked me if I'd like to see a show and have dinner in London. How could I refuse? I had been so lonely these passed weeks. I only had Bill to call me. So I accepted Ed's kind invitation.

We had a great time together. We didn't get into a show, but had a lovely dinner. Ed dropped me off at my front door as it was midnight and too late for him to come in for a cup of tea. I thanked him many times for his generosity. "I loved it Pat. We must do this again sometime." He drove away at a speed and was gone. I got quite a kick out of all this. Yet Ed wasn't a handsome man, but he had an attraction for me in some way. He was a man you had to know a while before you really liked him. It seemed easy for me to like him. Somehow we had many things in common. Ed had become like one of the family. He would drop by and see me any hour of the day.

We were having a happy hour around four o'clock. Ed didn't drink much, nor did I those days, but we had got to the state of seeing life a bit differently. We were being drawn together more; no, not by the drinks we had. There was a genuine feeling between us. We talked about our past lives. He was very interested in mine. He said he loved to hear all my problems. Ed seemed to get more loving to me as we talked. He suddenly put his arms around me and gave me a big hug and yes, a kiss on the lips. As we sat there time didn't seem to matter. We just went on holding hands and an occasional kiss. We didn't say much. We just smiled sweetly at each other. Ed seemed a different kind of man than I had known over a long period of years. He was different. We enjoyed each other in a sensible way, if there is such a thing.

I got looking forward to his visits. Ed was fond of fishing. He often went with a gentleman friend who had a boat and they would spend a few days at sea fishing. I was invited to make a trip with them. Ed arranged all the food for the trip, which lasted three days. I was pleased it was a fairly big boat. I always said I would never sail on a boat smaller than the Queen Mary, because I can't swim and I am afraid of water. This boat could hold 10 people, it had everything.

Ed's friend who owned the boat was a bachelor. He had been divorced just a year. He had one son who was in boarding school. We had three wonderful days. The boys had a good catch and the ocean was kind to us. Ed had a big freezer in his garage and it was full of all kinds of fish. He mostly lived on fish, we had many fish dinners together. Ed was a great cook, better than I.

After being away for three days I got a phone call from Bill and two cables lay on the floor near my mail. I was shocked to read the cables to tell me Bill was on his way over to see me to get the final answer from me, yes or no. He phoned me when he landed in London. He still wanted me to say yes. "Bill, can't you wait a little longer?"

"No, Pat, it's now or never."

That really hit me hard. Now that Ed had turned up in my life it was making it difficult to say yes to Bill. I seemed to love them both. I had lost interest in Bill as he was far away from me. Ed was here with me every day. Bill would arrive within 24 hours. I didn't know if I should let him stay with me. Ed wouldn't like it. I needed some help with this problem. Should I ask Ed what he thinks? I decided to call him. He really was surprised at the idea of Bill staying with me. I guess he thought he was the only one that mattered I my life. We talked it over and we came to realise that would be the only thing I could do, just let Bill stay with me for a few days. Ed said he would keep an eye on me while Bill was here. I knew Bill wouldn't like Ed hanging around as they are two different types of men.

Bill arrived on time. He was so happy to see me again. After a cup of tea we sat and talked and talked, but it didn't come round to asking me my decision as regards our marriage, a yes or no. Bill said he was flying to Bermuda for one weeks business trip and would I go along with him. This was a bigger problem for me to say yes. I dared to say, "Bill, I am sorry I can't go with you as I have a friend who arrives from Scotland any day, and she will be staying for a few weeks. I thought that would convince him that was the truth, but I saw that look in his eyes. He didn't understand me. He even suggested I could bring my lady friend along too. I told him that wouldn't work out, so Bill took off to Bermuda on his own, with no answer from me, yes or no.

Ed never had the chance to meet Bill. I was glad about that. He was pleased Bill had gone, as he liked to think he was the only man in my life. Of that I was not sure. I seemed to be very confused in the past few days. I felt I couldn't marry Ed, although he was a wonderful man. But I didn't think I could live with him for ever. I wanted to stay as we were, just lovers. I didn't think he would accept that. I tried to keep him from thinking of marriage to me yet. I could see he would one day want me to marry him.

I had a call from one of my tenants. It was Al, the doctor. He was having trouble with the shower in the bathroom. I went over to see what was the trouble. I showed him how it worked, so it was OK. He then asked me if I'd have a drink with him. Yes, I accepted a cup of tea, as it was early in the afternoon. We sat and he told me about his divorce. I thought it was strange for a doctor to live alone at his age. I resumed he must have been in his fifties. "I guess you are a busy man."

"Yes I am, but I make time for plenty of fun. Life would be too dull for a doctor if he didn't get satisfactions other than from his profession." I agreed with him. He asked me why I had not married. I told him it was too long a story to tell him then. "Maybe, Mrs. Armstrong, you will pay me a visit sometime when it's more convenient for both of us, and you can stay longer, maybe have dinner with me. I can cook a nice meal."

I returned the thanks. "Maybe I will when you aren't too busy."

I didn't think much of his invitation. I reckon he was being polite to me. Al was very tall. He must have been almost seven feet tall. He had quite a good opinion of himself. He always had a bunch of keys hanging from his belt. He would put them in his left pants pocket.

He said it added to his profile and it kept the ladies guessing. What an idea?

Al said he had been married to a gal four feet four, who was difficult to get on with. I told him a four feet four gal would be difficult to get on with. You would manage all right, but you wouldn't have anyone to talk to. We see many tall men married to small gals, but they still manage to have fun.

I hadn't heard from Bill since he left for Bermuda two weeks before. I was feeling kind of worried. Maybe he had given up for ever getting an answer from me. I could not blame him. He must have been suspicious of another lover hanging around me. I hated to do this to Bill. I couldn't bring myself to believe I could live with him for ever.

It was now six weeks since I heard from Bill. He must be back home now. Maybe he had met someone he liked better than me. It sounded like I was getting jealous of Bill. I couldn't wait any longer. I had to phone him. His housekeeper answered the phone. "Hello, this is Pat. Is Bill there?"

"No, he isn't." Came a quick reply, "Bill is in hospital again." That took me breath away.

"Please tell me Bess, how is Bill? What happened?"

"He was doing some repair work on the roof of his apartment. He was on a high ladder and it slipped from under him. He broke his leg and arm. He will be in the hospital for a few weeks; I'm sure of that, Pat." Bess gave me the phone number of the hospital. Immediately I phoned there but couldn't get a reply. I really got desperate. I must see Bill. I knew he wanted me at his side just now; I felt it was my duty to him.

I was on the plane at six o'clock that very day. I had no time to tell Ed. I thought I'd call him when I landed in New York. This was the worst flight I'd ever made. Bill was on my mind all the way. The stewardess was kind to me, and so was the gent who sat next to me. He told me he was going to the Bronx and if I wanted to accept his offer he would take me to Bill's apartment. I was so thankful and accepted his kind offer.

When we arrived, his car was waiting for us at the airport. I was so grateful to him. He drove me right to Bill's apartment. I didn't know his name. He handed me his card and said if he could be of any help, there was his phone number. "I'll be glad to help you."

I thanked him many times and said goodbye to him. By the time I got out of the car, Bess was there waiting for me. She had called a cab and off I went to the hospital; just about two miles away.

As I walked into a private room I could see one leg hanging way up in the air. I couldn't see Bill for bandages. "Bill darling, what are you doing here? I haven't heard from you for six weeks." Bill looked pale and didn't feel like talking. He didn't seem to know me at first sight. The all at once his face lit up with a big smile.

"Pat, my darling, you are here with me for ever." I didn't answer that but gave him a big kiss and a hug. I stayed one hour. I talked to the doctor and he said Bill would be home in two weeks.

Bill kept saying, "Pat, please stay here until I can get home." I promised him I would and left in a cab for his apartment. Bess was anxious to see me. We had a cup of tea and talked for a while. I didn't sleep much that night. I felt so lonely without Bill.

I was pleased one of Bill's tenants took me to the hospital every day. He was a godsend for me. He took me out for dinner several times. I got to know him as Bert. He didn't come in to see Bill. I thought that was funny. Bill asked me who brought me to the hospital. I had to tell him his name was Bert, one of his tenants. Bill gave me a funny look. I wondered why. However Bert did come in to see Bill on his day in the hospital. I noticed Bill shook his hand and called him Mr. Howorth, not Bert. I guessed they were not too friendly.

Bert was a very good kind of fellow in his sixties. I presumed he was a lady killer. Bill didn't seem to like him driving me to the hospital, etc. I didn't tell Bill we had been out for dinner together. That he wouldn't approve.

Bill came home. He had a nurse to care for him for several weeks. There was no mention of when I was to return home. Only, Bill would remark, "Darling, I need you; please stay with me." He would not hear of me leaving him now.

The weeks went by so quickly. I'd been there 10 weeks. Bill was doing fine but was a little pale. I could read his mind. He was waiting for me to say I was returning home soon. I hated to say this to him but with due respect to Ed I really must return home soon. I had not phoned Ed from New York as promised. I knew Ed would be worrying about me, so I decided to leave. It was a sad parting for Bill. I promised I would return again soon. Bill kept reminding me that this was my home when I was ready to stay with him. I felt I didn't want to leave him.

Bert took me to the airport. I thanked him and as I was leaving he bent over me and gave me a real soul devouring kiss on my lips. It really took me breath away. Then I heard him say, "Pat, forgive me for this, but I seem to have fallen in love with you. I can't understand why, because I know you belong to Bill just now." I couldn't understand all this as I had not given him any reason for it. He had treated me as a lady friend of Bill's. Now I could see why Bill wasn't pleased that Mr. Howorth was taking over the position.

I was happy to get on the plane for home. I was looking in my handbag and came across the card from the gentleman who sat next to me in the plane going to see Bill. He lived in the Bronx. I had not read the card but at the time he said I should call him Frank. He was an Englishman. His full name was Frank Holden, in Real Estate and he had a Bronx address. I would keep his card. I might need him again. He knew me as Pat Armstrong, living in the south of England, no address.

When I landed at the airport I was hoping someone would be there to meet me. I had not phoned Ed, so he wouldn't be there. I was about to hail a cab when I heard someone shouting so loud, "Hey, Pat, It's me. Can I help you? I am going your way now; I can drop you off at your home." No, it was not Ed, to my disappointment. It was Mr. Blair, one of my tenants. He said he had just flown in from Paris on a business trip. I didn't know him well enough for him to call me Pat. He said he was too excited at seeing me; he forgot my surname. He apologised, but I said I didn't mind him calling me Pat. I thanked him for the ride home.

The house seemed so empty, no one there to greet me. Where was Ed? He never had let me down. I guess he didn't know I was coming home. I still had Bill on my mind. I felt I should not have left him so soon. I had grown to love him more since his accident.

I promised I'd call him when I arrived home, but I must call Ed first. When he answered the phone he didn't greet me in his usual way. But he did enquire if I was all right. He never mentioned Bill. He sure was cool with me. Well, I guess that's it. Ed won't stand for that kind of treatment. It seems like I've lost a dear friend in Ed. I did apologise for not phoning from New York, but he didn't seem to want any apology from me. I told him I hadn't unpacked yet and that I would call him later on. I didn't say what time I would call him. I was so busy

I forgot. The days passed and I still did not call him. I thought I'd let him call me.

It was two weeks since I had talked to Ed. Well, if he didn't call me I would just let him go out of my mind. After all, Bill was my main worry just then. I knew I would miss Ed. He had never given me any ideas of marriage, so he had no claim on me.

Later on the phone rang. This must be Ed. I was hoping so. No, it wasn't. It was Fred, the new manager of the pub I used to work for. He called to ask if I could help him out for a couple of evenings. "I'd be delighted, Fred." This was the answer to my loneliness and would break the monotony for me.

I always walked to the pub. I enjoyed the walk. Who should I meet but Ed. He greeted me very friendly. It surprised me. He asked me if he could give me a lift. His car was just nearby. I told him I was going to help out at the pub for a couple of days. I thanked him for his kind offer, but I was very busy in the pub now. He quickly replied, "I'll walk with you, Pat, as I have nothing to do just now." He came into the pub and stayed all evening until it was closing time. He then insisted he would take me home in his car. I was thankful for that offer as the nights were getting darker.

When we arrived at my apartment, I asked the usual, "Are you coming in for a cuppa?" To my surprise he refused.

"No thanks, dear. I'll be getting along home as I have to take Rip for a walk." So that was good night. He sure was cool with me, not the Ed I used to know. Well, I was not going on my knees for any fellow. Ed would be back before long; I was sure of that.

The second night Ed came in we had a party going on upstairs in the club room. It was belonging to the Free Masons. They were mostly business men from London. They seemed to be in a happy mood. I got talking to one gentleman and he told me quite an interesting story. He had been married to one of England's Prime Minister's daughters. She had died two years ago. He looked to be a fellow in his fifties, maybe a bit more, but quite a charmer. He had too many drinks and I think that caused him to talk about his wife. He was a jolly sort of fellow. I liked his type. He seemed to want to keep on talking to me, but it was closing time so I had to excuse myself. He handed me his card and asked me to call him sometime when I was in London. I promised I would, and he just said good night. I never gave him another thought. I knew people who drank too much were different when they were sober. Who isn't?

Right now I had Ed on my mind and Bill too, so I couldn't give anyone else a thought. The third nigh I was in the pub Ed came in just before closing time. I was very busy and I didn't get the chance to talk to him. We closed the pub. Everyone was out, including Ed. I didn't know where he had gone. Fred, the manager, said, "Pat, I'll take you home. It's too late for you to walk home alone." I accepted that offer. He walked with me to my home. It was a lovely night. The moon was just coming to the full. I used to hate that same moon when it was at the full, as I knew I'd be bailing an alcoholic out of jail. But now I loved that same moon. It had changed my love life. I got so romantic, I just wanted to be loved, and loved.

That was what I needed so much, but I was with the wrong man. I didn't know Fred and besides I knew he was happily married. I had never been guilty of stealing someone's husband. I really enjoyed the walk home. We walked along the promenade and the reflection of the moon on the ocean made me think of Bill. He was so far away when I needed him.

Fred said goodnight and I thanked him. As I turned to walk up the three steps to my front door, there stood Ed. He had been waiting for me. "Hello there, Pat. It's me, Ed. I am sorry I missed you Pat. I wanted to walk you home from the pub." Ed didn't need any asking to come in for a cup of tea. He was in my house so quickly. We had tea on the veranda overlooking the ocean. Now the moon was slowly fading away. I felt like weeping. I felt I had been robbed of a beautiful lovable night. I was sure I could have made love to a lamp post just because of that full moon. How it affects people differently! I had Ed here with me but that didn't answer any of my problems. It was Bill on my mind all the time. What a way to spend an evening. Ed had never proved his love or his manhood to me. Bill was so different. He was the only fellow I had ever known who knew how to deal with a woman in love with love. I think a man is clever if he knows just what a woman needs and when she needs him. Bill did. I seemed to be missing him more than ever.

Ed and I sat talking until 2:00 am. I couldn't remember what we were trying to tell each other. Whatever he said to me didn't impress me at all. With Bill on my mind, how could he love me? I guess it was unfair of me as Ed had always been a gentleman to me in his own way. One doesn't meet a man like that very often. Some woman would adore him.

Ed suddenly decided to say goodnight. He just kissed me and that was the end of a beautiful unfulfilled night for me. He said he would call me the next day sometime. Ed made me think it was by choice he didn't want to love me, or maybe it was a thing of the past for him. Ed wasn't that old, a man in his sixties, I presumed. Maybe this was the reason Ed had never offered me marriage. I went to bed just to dream about Bill. I'll call him tomorrow, I thought. I can't go on without him any longer.

Ed was round the next day to see me again to say he was taking a holiday. He thought he needed one badly. "What about it, Pat; will you come with me?" Well, that was a sudden question to answer just then.

"Where are you going Ed?"

"Where do you want to go dear? You name the place and we will go." I could have said the USA to see Bill, but that would be unkind.

"What about the Isle of Man, an island off the west coast just five hours sailing? We can fish, gamble and take lovely walks on the island." "That sounds great. Let's go. When can you be ready, Pat. Two days?"

"Yes, I'll be ready."

We went by boat. I prefer it to flying. Ed had already booked our hotel accommodation. It was a very nice ocean front modern hotel. We had a suite of rooms overlooking the ocean. The weather was perfect. Our bedrooms adjoined the lounge.

The first night we were there we went to the dog races. This brought back memories of the two dogs I once owned. I'd called them Molly and Martha, but never won a race if I remember right. I looked at the program and saw one dog was called Bill the Kid. It was the favourite too. I had to back it for Bill's sake. Ed gave me a funny look when I had decided to back a dog with a name like that., so Ed decided he would back it too, and it won by three lengths. We had a lucky night; we backed five winners.

WE were both feeling tired. We'd had a busy day, so we both went to bed early, with just a peck on the cheek from Ed, "Goodnight, dear."

I didn't sleep too well. My mind was on Bill, as usual. I awoke about 7:00 am. I hadn't seen Ed yet; maybe he was still sleeping. I opened his bedroom door and no Ed. How funny I thought. Where is he? I was worried about him because I knew he loved to swim.

It was 8:30 now. I had showered and dressed and the maid brought in a nice cup of tea, which I really needed. At 9:00 o'clock Ed walked in. I was relieved to see him. "Where have you been, Ed?"

"Darling," he replied, "I just did my usual."

"What's that?" I was anxious to know.

"I always go to 7:00 o'clock Mass every day of my life, Pat. I forgot to tell you." I didn't even know he was a Catholic.

The maid brought in our breakfast. I told Ed I had my own religion too, but I was not against anyone else's beliefs. "I would have gone with you Ed." He was surprise at me saying that. But I could never become a Catholic. I told Ed my sister was a Catholic for 26 years and changed to a more simple religion. I had a dear friend, a Catholic Priest, whom I wrote to often. We were kids together.

After breakfast we sat in the lounge. Ed didn't try to convert me to being a Catholic. He knew I was not interested. He would be wasting is time. Ed was not a fanatic about his religion. He would tell me jokes that were near the knuckle. He once told me a story about a priest who was taking his morning ride on his bicycle. He was coming down a bit too fast and at the corner of the street he collided with another gentleman one his bicycle. He turned out to be a Church of England Minister. They both blamed each other for the collision. The English Minister said to the Irish Priest, "But for my cloth, I'd give you a good whipping."

The Priest said in return, "Sure and begorrah, if it wasn't a Friday I'd chew your blooming ears off." (I think he said balls). I guess Catholics don't eat meat on Fridays. Or do they?

Now I realised why Ed hadn't asked me to marry him. He knew I wouldn't take his religion. We had a nice holiday together. I don't think it helped either of us. It didn't bring us any closer, but we remained good friends.

When I arrived home, I immediately phoned Bill to see how he was. He was thrilled to hear my voice again. Then he asked me the usual question, "When, my love, are you coming back to the USA?"

I quickly answered, "Bill, darling, I can't just now. I have just joined a thrift shop for retarded children. I do two days a week." This did not seem to convince Bill one bit. I guess he thought it was just an excuse I was making.

He was quiet for a few moments; then he burst forth with, "Darling, I have a surprise for you." That kind of shocked me for a moment. I guess I had kept him waiting too long for my answer. He continued to say, I have decided to sell up and go and live in California." I couldn't believe my ears. I asked him to repeat it. Well, I was surprised but very happy to hear it. I had to say I was glad he had decided on California. Bill said his health had deteriorated the past few months and he thought Californis sunshine would help him.

"When will all this happen, Bill?"

"Just as soon as I can sell all my property here." That sure was a surprise for me. I wished him luck with all his sales, as property was going higher every year.

It seemed to me Bill was sick of waiting for my answer to marry him. This, I presumed, had made him decide to go to California. This might interest me more than to live in the Bronx. We talked for quite a while and he said he would let me know when he arrived in California. He just said, "Bye, darling; I'll see you in California."

Chapter Eight.

I didn't tell Ed, he wouldn't be interested.

I was hanging my clothes up I the closet and I noticed a card had dropped out of one of my pockets. I read it and to my surprise it was given to me by a gentleman who was at the Freemason dinner party some weeks past. It seems it was a London address. The Globe Clothing Manufacturers, President/Owner, Harry J. McDonald, phone 444-6541. I remembered him. He was a very talkative person. He asked me to phone him if I was in London any time. I suddenly thought he would be the man who could help our thrift shop. I wondered if I dared phone him. Why not? I really took a big chance of a refusal. His secretary answered my call and asked my name and my business. I told her it was a private call. "Just say it's Pat calling from the coast." After waiting several minutes he came on. Again I said I was Pat from the coast. He immediately knew when I spoke to him who I was.

"Yes, dear, I know you, Pat. How nice of you to call me. Where are you, Pat? Let's have a coffee somewhere." I had to tell him I was phoning from the coast where I lived. I tried to tell him the reason I had phoned him, but he was too eager to try to make a date with me. However, when I told him I needed some clothes or furniture for our thrift shop and I thought he could help me, he quickly replied, "Pat, you are asking the right person. I can help you." He said he was in touch with a lot of business people who often gave to these thrift shops. "Why don't you come and have dinner with me tomorrow?" That I promised. Harry met me at the station. He looked a different type of man from the night I met him. He had been drinking too much at the party. He was a very attractive man. I was so happy to meet him again. It was Pat and Harry now. As we picked up his car I was surprised to see it was this years model, a Bentley. Money seemed to speak here.

Harry took me to one of London's posh restaurants somewhere near Piccadilly. We had a wonderful meal. It was nearly 8:00 o'clock. We had talked quite a bit about his affairs. He said his wife was divorcing him after 25 years of marriage. I had to say I was sorry to hear this, but it didn't seem to bother him; he was a happy-go-lucky kind of fellow. That put me at ease with him.

We drove around London as my train time wasn't till 10:15.
"Pat, why can't I drive you home? I have time on my hands and it's
only 8:00 clock."

"OK. That suits me Harry."

We arrived at home an hour later. That car really could go. I
enjoyed the ride. I asked him to come in for a cup of tea. Harry
jumped at the chance. Before I made our tea the phone rang. I thought,
Oh, this must be about Bill. But, no. One of my tenants called to say
he was called to Scotland. He had to leave early in the morning. It was
urgent family business. He was moving out in the next two days. A
van would be coming to collect his furniture.

It was a beautiful night so we sat on the veranda watching the
moon on the ocean and talking about our lives. Harry's business was
very successful. His father had started it in a small kind of way. Harry
built it up when he took over. He told me he was very sad his wife was
divorcing him. It was only after they had been married for a few years
they found they both wanted different things from life. I told him I
sure found that out.

The stuff for the thrift shop was going to arrive in a day or so.
One of Harry's vans was going to collect from his friends. When his
wife moved out she left some clothes behind. He said they would be
coming too. I thanked him for all that. Harry said they often had
clothes models wore. They couldn't sell them for new but were OK for
a thrift shop.

Harry told me how much he enjoyed looking out over the
ocean. He said it relaxed him. Harry had always wanted to live at the
coast but his wife was a town person and wouldn't move. He said this
was what he needed after a busy day at work. I thought Harry was just
the kind of fellow to brighten up my life, so I told him about the phone
call. "Pat," he said, "that apartment would suit me down to the ground.
It's just what I need." I could see Harry was a quick worker. He said
we should celebrate his new apartment. I had a bottle of wine and said
that would be better than tea. "That would be a perfect end to a perfect
day." Another lady killer?

The moon moved across the sky and we talked until the early
hours. The wine was finished about 3:00 am, and so were we. Harry
left for London after all the excitement. He waved bye bye and said,
"I'll see you soon, dear."

I was in the shop the day after these goods came in. I was
surprised at the lovely ladies clothes and handbags. The manager was

delighted with all these goodies. She sent him a thank you note. We got to work to hang these clothes up and mark the prices. Harry's wife must have been a very extravagant person. These clothes were very expensive.

As we went through these clothes we always looked into the pockets and in the handbags for anything that could be left in by mistake. We often found money. We didn't find any money, but I found an unopened letter that was addressed to Harry. I immediately put it in my pocket before anyone could see me. I'd keep it until I saw Harry again. I didn't open it. I could have as it wasn't sealed. I often wondered what could be said in it and why did she write to Harry and forget to post it? This was a strange ting to happen to me. I wished I hadn't found it, but I'd give it to Harry when he moved in here.

I didn't see Harry for two weeks until he moved in. He was surprised when I gave him the letter I found in his wife's purse. He didn't say anything. He just put it in his pocket. I didn't ask any questions.

It took a few weeks for Harry to get settled in his new apartment. All the furniture he bought was beautiful and went well with the apartment. His Bentley car was a tight fit for the garage, but it went in OK.

I hadn't seen Ed to tell him about Harry moving into that apartment. He might have phoned me while I was working at the shop.

I did get a call from Bill to say he had changed his mind about California and decided not to sell his property in the Bronx. Then in the next breath he said he had bought four apartments in Palm Springs. I just couldn't understand him. He seemed all mixed up. "Bill, please now tell me, are you going to live in Palm Springs? That's California."

"Oh yes, dear, I do intend to live in Palm Springs." Well, now I knew. I didn't know what to say now. I told him he was wise not to sell his property in the Bronx as the prices would go much higher in the next year or so.

Bill said he was buying new furniture for his Palm Springs apartments. We didn't talk for long. He said he would call me when he got settled in Palm Springs.

Harry was very happy in his apartment. He invited me in for dinner. Some men are good cooks and he cooked a delicious dinner. We had champagne to celebrate his new home.

I was amazed to see his king sized bed. It made me wonder why a king size? He said he had just bought it. He wasn't that big.

Tall, but slim. I guess he was an opportunistic fellow. He probably thought it was going to be used by some beautiful blonde gal. I guess he was right. He wasn't the type who would marry again, although he would be a good catch for someone.

Harry treated me like a lady all the time I was in his apartment. I thanked him for his generosity and the lovely meal he cooked, as I left him with no problems. Harry reminded me to come back soon. That I promised him. I liked his manners. He knew how to please a lady. Up to this point he was my choice.

Ed called me to say his dog had died. I was sorry to hear that. He was a sweet old dog. One can expect this to happen. Ed had not mentioned his son recently. I resumed he was still in a wheelchair from that terrible accident. I didn't like to ask questions. When I was there some weeks past his son wasn't there. Maybe he was having some kind of treatment at a hospital.

I asked Ed to come around to have dinner with me. I had to admit it was my turn for dinner. He arrived about 4:00 o'clock. He didn't seem as perky as he usually had been. We had a nice dinner together but over the meal Ed would give me funny glances, a strange look on his face. I could see there was something on his mind. I had to ask him if he was feeling all right. He looked at me and said, "Why do you ask dear? I am just fine." But I could see the difference since I last saw him. I didn't press him for the truth.

Later in the evening we were sitting having coffee and here he told me a sad story. He had to go into hospital as soon as he could. His doctor had told him he had cancer of the bowels. "Ed, darling, I am just shocked at this news, but I know you will be all right after the operation." That had really upset me, although I could see Ed had not looked too well these past months.

Ed went into the hospital just a couple of days later. I didn't visit him for a few days. I asked his doctor to let me know the results, so I had to wait to hear from him. I talked to his doctor before he was to have the operation and he told me he was not too happy about Ed's condition. It was one of those 50/50 operations. I didn't know if Ed knew this. I told him I had talked to his doctor.

Ed reminded me that I would look after his property etc. Yes, I promised everything would be cared for until he came home again. Ed was operated on at 9:00 clock. I called the hospital at 10:00, but no news yet, only that he was in the intensive care unit. I was praying he would be all right. He was too young to die, he was only 59.

As the days went by he was slowly getting better, but he could have no visitors yet. I was longing to see him. I was not allowed to phone him.

After two weeks I could visit Ed. He was so happy to see me. I could see he was failing in health. I held his hand and said a prayer for him. He didn't look like Ed at all. It came to my mind, who was going to look after him when he came home? I was only allowed five minutes with him. That was enough for me. I was deeply sorry for Ed.

When I arrived home I got a phone call from the hospital to say Ed had collapsed and died of heart failure a few minutes after I had left him. I called the doctor and he said it was a hopeless case. He couldn't do anything for him. I was in a state of shock for weeks. I told Harry all about it and he was very kind to me. Ed was the nicest fellow I ever knew. I would miss him a lot. This was another closed book for me. I never found out what happened to his son.

I had an unexpected call from a fellow I had nearly forgotten. It was from a Mr. Howorth. He said he was on a visit to England and he wanted to say hello to me. I just couldn't place him at all. "Who are you?" I enquired.

His reply was, "Pat, dear, don't you remember me? I am Bert from the Bronx, the fellow who took you to see Bill when he was in hospital."

Oh, my goodness, that was a surprise. He was the fellow whom Bill didn't care much for. I asked him where he was phoning from and could I help him? He had arrived from the USA the day before he phoned me and was staying in London for a few days. He was going to Scotland on a business trip. I invited him to have dinner with me on his way up to Scotland. I felt I had to return his kindness to me when Bill was in the hospital, but he refused and insisted he would take me out for dinner.

We had several nights out together. He told me a lot about Bill, which I didn't like. I didn't attach any importance to what he said, only that Bill had decided to live in Palm Springs. Bert was very disappointed at Bill leaving the Bronx and was glad he wasn't going to sell his apartments in the Bronx.

I was still feeling sad about the great loss of Ed. Bert asked me if I would go up to Scotland with him for a few days. I did need this break, so I said, "I'd love to, Bert."

Bert stayed with me a couple of nights and we took my car and drove up to Scotland. I didn't use it much these days. We broke out journey half way up to Scotland and stayed in a little country pub. Bert was great to me, no messing about at all. I was in no mood for it anyway.

We stayed in Edinburgh two nights, and then on to Glasgow. I did some shopping. We decided we would drive back on the east coast road, and down through Alnwick where I used to live. We stayed there one night at the pub. I had many memories, not too nice ones at times, but remembrances of the dances we had at the castle. That I'll never forget. That seemed a lifetime away. So much had happened to me since then.

We were having a drink after our dinner and a tall gentleman with slightly grey hair came across to us and excused himself for doing this, "But, aren't you Pat?" I looked at him and I just couldn't think where I had met him. He must have been an Alnwick fellow. My brains didn't seem to work just then.

"You'll have to tell me who you are. I can't place you."

"Now, Pat, you must remember that night after the dance at the castle. I walked home with you and Betty." Oh, I knew now who he was. I was glad he didn't tell the whole story. It was pretty grim. That was the night we found my husband lying dead drunk in the pathway of our house. He helped me to get him to bed. That was a fearful night for me. But, we changed the subject and he shook hands and left us. I was happy about that. Bert was very understanding regarding this.

We left Alnwick the morning after. We were blessed with good weather all the way home. We had two stops before we got to my home. Bert stayed with me for three nights before flying off to the Bronx. He was a very interesting fellow. He had never told me all this before, when I was in the Bronx. It was a very interesting story. He said he'd never been married. He must have been around 50, but he had lived with an English girl fore five years, and she left him to go back to England and never returned to him. He said he was very fond of her and he had not met anyone else since that he could spend some of his life with. He continued to tell me he had lived with a dear friend for about three years. He was a she man. Bert didn't quite admit he had practiced homosexuality, but I presumed so. I guess he had no more interest in women after that experience.

Well, I had to say this about Bert, he was a perfect gentleman to me, and I enjoyed his company. I wouldn't have thought he was a man who had practiced homosexuality, but one can never tell these days. They are very charming fellows to know, as I have known a lot of them. It kind of struck me as funny. I wondered if Bill knew this about Bert, maybe not. I would never mention this to Bill. I understand a lot of men have practiced this some time in their lives. It's as well we women don't know about this. I guess many people keep or practice the Eleventh Commandment - 'Thou shalt not be found out'.

We arrived home after a nice holiday. Bert flew off back to the Bronx two days later. I said, "Give my love to Bill. Tell him I'll be seeing him soon." Bert thanked me and asked me to forget all the stories he had told me regarding his past life. I said, "Don't worry Bert, I am used to meeting people like you."

The morning after I got home, Harry knocked on my door. He was concerned as he hadn't seen me for nearly a week, and was I all right? "Oh, come in Harry, I have been up to Scotland for a week."

He replied, "I have missed you, Pat," and gave me a big hug. I enjoyed seeing Harry again. He had a nice lovable way with him, but never took advantage of a big hug. He seemed to know how to deal with the ladies.

"How do you like your apartment Harry?"

"Oh, I just love it. I hope I can live here for ever." It's strange, Harry never mentioned the letter I had found in his wife's handbag. Maybe one day he would tell me. I wouldn't ask him; I wouldn't hurt his feelings, he was too nice a fellow, and I had grown to respect him, maybe to love him one day, who knows? My love life now had been sadly neglected. I missed Bill so much. Harry seemed to have taken Bill's place those past few weeks, in a way. He was so kind to me. He was the type that wouldn't buy his love life, he'd have to love her truly. I believed that to be true about Harry and with Bill. I had a strong affection for both these men. They had the same principles on life and love.

Harry stayed for nearly an hour. I seemed to be content for him to stay longer, but he was going up to town and would not be back for two nights. He said he would call me. Harry got on very well with the doctor upstairs, but neither had much time for the other. I am glad for that as it would take Harry away from me. I was missing Ed these days. I knew Harry had been a blessing for me in a way, he came when Ed passed away.

Harry's divorce was all settled. He was a free man again. He called me to come up to London for a dinner and show to celebrate his being a bachelor again. Mr. Hanson, my tenant, took me to the station, and Harry met me in London. He seemed full of the joys of spring. He was just walking on air. I said to him, "Harry, you seem so happy tonight."

He said, "I couldn't be any happier with anyone else in the world." That was a strong statement to make. I wondered if he really meant it.

Harry proved to me later in the evening how much he thought of me. Maybe I shouldn't take him seriously as it could be a rebound from his divorce. We had a lovely meal, but too late for a show, so we came home. He came in for a drink and we talked till midnight. He hadn't told me much about his business. It was a very prosperous affair. He still didn't say anything about the letter. I was surprised to hear they had an adopted daughter. She was 21 and had recently married. I thought he said he had no children of his own. It seems they were told the first two years of their marriage she couldn't have children. That was a blow to Harry as he loved children.

We got on talking about religion. He said he had none. "But you must have," I said. He said he was brought up as a Baptist, but he didn't agree with it later on in life. He said he had a brother who was a minister whom he had not seen for many years. I didn't seem to be able to draw him out to tell me more about himself. I thought that was strange. I thought I'd better not pursue it.

I thanked him for a lovely evening. He remarked it was a great pleasure for him. "I'll call you tomorrow, Pat." I went to bed that night just thinking, what's his problem? He must have some.

I was still waiting to hear from Bill. I expected he was busy moving. I got a call from Bert. He said Bill was in Palm Springs.

I had a call from the thrift shop to ask if I'd go in, the manageress was off sick. I was always glad he did say she was divorced and had no children. I was very interested in Marie. I got quite friendly with her later. She would come and spend a whole day with me, and often we went out for lunch. She kind of grew on me in that she seemed to have had the same kind of life that I'd had many years ago.

She told me she lived alone in an apartment just along the promenade. She asked me for dinner one evening. I was really surprised to see her beautiful home, most expensive furniture and valuable antiques. She started to tell me where she had bought them.

She sure was a good cook. We had wine with our meal. We drank quite a bit between us. As the evening went on we were full of sympathy for each other regarding our early years. She told me the most incredible stories I've ever heard in my life. She had lived with three different men before she married. All these men were either not married or divorced. She remarked to me that she had never taken on a married man. She was brought up a Catholic, but not any more. It seems her mother had never been married. She lived with some fellow whom Marie thought was her father. As Marie got older she took on the same kind of living as her mother, but was more successful financially.

I was feeling sorry for Marie. She had earned all the things she had. I didn't tell her much of my past life, as she was too busy talking about hers.

I didn't know her surname yet, as it was always Marie. One day at the store I was looking through the books where we all had to sign, and there was Marie Hall written down. Gee, that sounded familiar. Oh no, it couldn't be! Her name was Hall. Gosh, I thought that was Ed's name. No, I thought, it couldn't be, as Ed had one son, and Marie said she had no other children. Well, I guess I must go slower.

When the manageress came back to work, I got talking to her about Marie, and she told me Marie was married to a prosperous businessman for a number of years, and then found out he had been unfaithful to her, so she divorced him. But they did adopt a boy of 12 that she hadn't seen for years. This story was coming to my mind that it must have been Ed's wife.

After this I cooled off with Marie. I didn't want to get involved with her and Ed. Yes, the truth came out. She was Ed's wife. She hadn't seen him for many years. What a small world, I thought. I didn't tell her I knew Ed. Marie had been living in the north of England and had just moved down here. We still were friends. I didn't encourage her to talk about Ed. I wanted to remember him as I knew him.

Well, I was still waiting to hear from Bill. I had a call from Harry as usual most every other day. I didn't seem to know what was on Harry's mind the other evening. Something was troubling him. Was it the letter, I thought. Maybe next time we are out for dinner he will tell me. Harry was only in his fifties, I presumed. Surely he had got past the stage of chasing blondes. A man worries about blondes when he is 40, and when he gets to be 60 he start worrying about his bowels. Maybe he was having trouble with his. I hoped not.

Harry called me to say he would be around that evening. I said to come and have dinner with me. OK, he replied, "I'll be around about 6:00." He arrived on time with a most beautiful bunch of flowers. I was so pleased to accept them.

After our meal we sat on the settee just relaxing. "Pat," he said, "I've got to tell someone this. Can I talk to you?"

"Harry," I said, "you know me. I'll be glad to listen. Can I help you in any way?"

"No, I don't think so, Pat. It is about the letter you found in my wife's handbag. That letter, Pat, wasn't written by my wife. It was from a lady friend of mine I'd had for a few months. She had written to my wife to say she was determined to get me by all means, as I had cooled off and didn't want any part of her again. She said in the letter she wasn't going to be thrown out so quickly by me. Pat, this woman has never left me alone. She phones and has threatened to shoot me one day. I just don't know what to do with her. Do you have any suggestions, Pat?"

This woman was in her fifties and had really fallen for Harry. She would go to his place of business and make a scene and Harry would have to take her out to lunch to quiet her.

"Harry, if I were you I would send her a lawyer's letter asking her to stop harassing you. That should do it".

Some weeks after Harry hadn't seen or heard from this woman, he opened the local paper and to his amazement her death was announced. She had been found shot and there was going to be an inquiry. This is what Harry was upset about. I was beginning to think some unkind things about Harry. I tried not to. I was very worried.

Harry was called as witness to the inquiry. He had to state his case. Harry told me not to worry as he had nothing to do with her being shot. The case went on for a few weeks. Thank goodness Harry was cleared of all guilt. What came to light was she did intend to shoot Harry one day and was handling the gun and accidentally shot herself. Harry was greatly relieved when the case was closed.

That was a frightening few weeks for both of us. I kept my fait in Harry. I couldn't believe he was guilty of such an act. It had put years on Harry. He was a different man now. Harry became so sick he had to rest a lot, so I didn't see him as often. He would call me and I could hear that his voice sounded so different.

I went over to see him. He was lying down and he was white as snow. I couldn't believe the difference in him. Within two weeks he had lost a lot of weight. I made him tempting meals that he didn't eat. At last he was taken to hospital with a serious case of malnutrition. He was in the hospital three weeks. He looked years older. I talked to his doctor and he told me it would take time for Harry to get back to normal.

Weeks went by. He returned home and was able to go to his business a few days a week.

I had a call from Bill. He was in Palm Springs now and he sounded very happy to live there. "When are you coming, Pat?" Well, I felt I needed a break after all the worry I'd had with Harry's case.

"Any time you want me to come," I quickly replied; "next week, Bill?"

"That's great. I'll meet you at L.A. Airport. Let me know your time and date you arrive."

I was so excited at the thought of seeing Bill again. I told Harry about my trip to California. He was very upset at the thought I would be away at least six weeks. He said he didn't know how he could live that long without me being near to him to comfort him. I thought Harry might get a shock when I returned. He took me to the airport. I just gave him a big hug. I noticed his eyes looked watery. "I'll be back, Harry. God bless you, darling." H waved me goodbye.

I got the feeling I wouldn't be seeing him again. There was something on his mind. I knew he had not told me all. I guess he will tell me when I return. I trust he was not involved with her death. This would be the biggest shock of my life, but it was not for me to judge him. To me he was a very fine person.

One never knows; some people have a Jeckal and Hyde personality. To me Harry was a good person. I would try to think kindly of him.

Chapter Nine.

I had a very pleasant flight over. I met some nice people in the first class lounge. One gentleman I met was returning to Los Angeles. I had a few drinks with him. He really got quite talkative and told me he had a chain of restaurants. I didn't ask him where, but he invited me to a free meal at any one of his restaurants. He gave me his card. I could hand it to the manger of any of these restaurants. I thanked him and told him I was bound for Palm Springs. "Oh, how nice; I have a house there. We are often there. I'd love you to call and see us one day." I promised I would, and he wrote down the address of his house in Palm Springs. I was wondering who the "we" were - I presumed his wife. I found out later it was his son, 17 years of age.

I went to the restroom for an excuse to re-read his card. He was Mr. P.H. Fleming of "Cracker Barrel" Restaurants, Inc., California. We really got very friendly on the nine-hour trip. He asked me to call him Philip. "I'd love to. I'm Pat from London; well, not far from London, just on the coast."

Philip was an easy fellow to get to know. He told me he lost his wife in a plane accident just 12 months before. He said they were a very devoted pair. I expressed my sorrow to him.

When the plane landed, he said, "Bye for now. I'll see you later." Gee, I thought, that sounds like he has made up his mind to see me in Palm Springs. I didn't give him my address where I was staying, but I did say I was staying with a friend of mine who had just bought four apartments in Palm Springs.

Bill was there waiting for me, frantically waving his hands. "Darling, am I glad to see you! I have been so lonely here."

I didn't know if I could stay here forever. We had a nice drive to Palm Springs and was it hot! - a bit too hot for me, but I guessed I'd get used to it.

We arrived at Bill's place. It was a ground floor lovely apartment. There was a swimming pool at his door. As we walked in, there was his housekeeper he had in the Bronx.

This was a big apartment. It was two apartments and Bill had it made into one large apartment, four bedrooms, two-and-a-half baths. It was just beautiful - all new furniture. Yes, and another king size bed. These men are very opportunistic!

I noticed Bill had a limp. I asked him how he was, but he didn't mention he was having trouble walking. I could see he was in pain. Bess, his housekeeper, had prepared a nice meal for us. It seemed so peaceful here, but hot. I really didn't like it so hot. I think that's what worried Bill right now, although there was air conditioning throughout the apartments.

Bess was flying back to the Bronx the day after I arrived. She was in charge of the apartments, so she had to get back.

Bill seemed to have changed his image on life. He was more content with less excitement. He was now 60, but he looked much older since his fall. I liked him better this way. I seemed to be getting there myself, but I still needed a lot of loving. I couldn't live without it.

Bill helped me unpack and showed me my bedroom. It was just heavenly. On the bed lay a baby doll night dress and a frilly gown to go with it. That's Bill; he never forgets one thing. He was making me love him more and more. But, I wondered if this was the Bill I knew before his accident. He had something that I never found in the other men I had met over the past years; it was always me first.

The first night we went for a swim. The mood was just coming to the full. We adjourned into the Jacuzzi. We seemed to be enjoying it when suddenly Bill was struck with a pain in the leg that had been broken earlier. I had a job to get him out of the water. I managed with the help of a neighbour gentleman. He was very kind to Bill. We got him in the house and I massaged his leg. He said it felt better. I took him to a local doctor and he advised Bill to just rest for a few days, so that's what we did. We spent our time lounging on the patio, drinking in the sunshine. I was beginning to get quite brown. Bill had a lovely tan.

This Mr. R. Williams, Bill's neighbour, came to see how he was. I noticed Bill called him Ray. They seemed very friendly. He made a habit of coming across to sit with us on Bill's patio, and he enjoyed a drink around 4:00 o'clock. He was quite a looker; he was well groomed, had a small beard and a moustache. I used to fall for men with a moustache - something about them that was different.

One day he brought a lady with him. "Meet my fiancée Liz." She looked to be about 38, a very sweet person, and of course she was a blonde with longish hair. Ray, I guessed, was at least 50. I was sure of that. As time went by we learned he was divorced and was living with Liz. Maybe he did intend to marry her one day.

Bill was feeling fine again. He suggested we make a trip to Los Angeles to do some shopping. I really didn't need a thing, but Bill would buy me jewellery. He had a craze for Jewellery. He wore a gold chain around his neck for years.

I didn't know what I wanted, but Bill knew I loved rings. He bought the most precious ring I'd ever seen - a rare sapphire. I didn't know much about these rare stones, but it was blue and very beautiful. "Bill, you spoil me," I remarked.

"Darling, you know I love you with all my heart." I'd never heard this coming from him before. I could see he meant every word of it. What could I say but only, "I love you too, Bill." The next thing I heard was, "Let's get married, darling." Oh my, he sounds like he really means it this time.

"Bill, please don't rush me; give me a few weeks to think it over." Bill suggested we should fly to Las Vegas for a quickie marriage. I really was flabbergasted. I kept thinking about Harry. Whatever would he do without me to tell his troubles to? I had not called or written to Harry and I didn't give him my address because Bill wouldn't like that.

Bill had to still rest a little, so we spent a lot of time on the patio. One afternoon, to my surprise, Philip turned up. I wondered how he got the address where I was staying. I introduced him to Bill as a friend I had met on the plane coming over. Philip was alone. We offered him a seat and a drink. He went on to say he lived only three houses down and he had seen Bill and me going out walking several times. So he thought he would come and say hello to us. I didn't think Bill was enjoying his company, as Philip was a bit of a blow bag. He was full of his own importance. However, Philip invited us over for cocktails the day after, and to my surprise, Bill graciously accepted the invite.

We kept our appointment with Philip. We just walked three houses down. My goodness, you wouldn't think there was a house behind that high wall and trees. We had never noticed this all the times we had walked past it. As we walked up a long drive, two great big Afghan dogs came running up to greet us. They were friendly, and Philip came out to meet us to show us the way in.

As we entered the house he introduced us to an elderly lady who was his mother. She was a sweet person. We sat out on the veranda. Philip just pushed a bell and the housemaid arrived dressed in cap and apron of coffee-coloured lace. She looked lovely. She was about in her thirties. Philip asked us what we would like to drink. "I just love champagne, Philip." Bill said something on the rocks. The maid appeared with the drinks and w sat there for two hours until it was getting time for dinner. Philip was telling us about all the restaurants he owned. He had one in Palm Springs. "Why don't we go there and have dinner?"

Bill immediately replied, "We would love to."

"OK, I'll see you both in half an hour. I'll pick you up in my car. It's not too far to go."

"Thanks a lot, Philip," I said.

We returned to Bill's place. We both got dressed for the occasion and Philip was on time to pick us up. Bill never said one word against my meeting Philip on the plane. He would never accuse me of flirting. I really didn't think I intended it to be that way with Philip. He didn't seem the kind who would.

Philip brought along his girlfriend Roz. She seemed very fond of Philip. We had a marvellous dinner with all the trimmings. Philip just knew the best kind of wines for our dinner.

I felt so happy to be with Bill again. I didn't know if it was the wine that was taking effect, but I was on the verge of accepting Bill's offer to marry him. As the evening grew on I calmed down more and forgot all about it.

Philip and Roz came over to Bill's place for drinks after dinner and they stayed until midnight, as it was a hot night - too warm to go to bed. And that beautiful moon was out at full now. I couldn't express my feelings when it was at full moon. I seemed to be a different person altogether. I think Bill knew this, as he was always especially nice to me.

I got to thinking if that king size bed would be used this night, but it was a real hot and humid night. I guessed not. We still sat there after Philip and Roz had gone home. I could see Bill had something on his mind, but I hoped it wasn't Las Vegas. I didn't think I should decide yet; somehow I had been thinking about Harry, wondering how he was. I couldn't get a chance to call him, as Bill was around all the time.

I asked Bill how his leg was. He didn't answer me until I asked him again. "Oh, it still hurts a little." But I could see he wasn't happy about it. I knew he did limp now and then. I didn't worry about it.

I had been with Bill nearly three weeks now. I thought I'd like to take a walk, but he didn't want to walk just then, so I went alone.

It wasn't very far to town. I thought I might phone Harry.

I managed to talk to Harry. He was so happy to hear from me. The first thing he asked me was, "When are you coming home, Pat? I am so lonely without you."

"Harry, I just can't say when yet, but I will let you know as soon as I can."

He replied with a strong voice, "Pat, you know I love you and I need you so badly right now. Please come home soon."

"Harry, I will let you know soon; 'bye for now." What else could I say? I wished I could make up my mind. It was Bill sometimes and Harry sometimes. I seemed to love them both. I must make up my mind pretty soon. I was sure Bill would be losing his patients with me soon. I kept putting him off. I may be pushing my luck too far one of these days. Then Bill will give me up altogether. I wouldn't like that to happen. I was very fond of him, although I found Bill had changed a lot since he had that accident. His manhood wasn't the same; even if we did marry I couldn't see that king size bed being used. I really couldn't bring myself to a marriage similar to the one that I had annulled many years ago. I was not a sex symbol, but I did need some loving sometimes. How could I tell this to Bill? I didn't want to hurt him.

One evening we had a serious talk. I suggested I would return home and I would think about it and make up my mind once and for all. I would have to sell all my property and belongings. "Bill, this will be a big decision for me to make, so please give me time."

"Darling, I can't wait any longer."

I gave him a pat on his hands and I said, "Bill, please give me time."

"OK. I'll give you just four weeks to decide when you get home."

I decided I would return home within the next three days. Bill would take me to the airport. We had dinner again with Philip and Roz before I left. The day before I was to fly off, Bill's leg was very painful and we took him to the doctor. We were shocked to hear Bill would have to return to the hospital for an adjustment on the leg, and he had to rest as much as he could. Philip was very kind to Bill and offered to take me to the airport. Bill didn't like the idea, but he accepted the offer. I felt so sorry I was leaving Bill when he really needed me, but I had been away six weeks now and I must go home. I was looking forward to seeing Harry.

Philip was very sweet to me. He helped me with my
luggage, came and sat with me until the plane was ready to fly off. He
told me he was due back in London again the following week, so I
invited him to come and have dinner with me. I thanked him and said
goodbye.

I had a pleasant journey home. Harry was right there waiting
for me at the airport. I really got a great thrill when I saw him standing
there. He looked a real gentleman. Well, that sure was a big hug from
him. I returned it by a kiss and thanked him for meeting me.
"Darling," he said, "I have been living for this hour to meet you again.
Are you here for good, Pat?" I didn't answer that. I just couldn't. He
didn't take me to my apartment, but said he had made a meal for me at
his place. Harry was a good cook and I enjoyed the meal he had made.

After dinner he took me home and helped me with the
unpacking of my luggage. I had quite a lot. I had bought him a shirt.
He liked the colours, quite gay looking. I wasn't sure if he liked gay
colours.

I was feeling tired after 10 hours on the plane. "Harry, please
forgive me, I feel I need some sleep."

"I'll see you in the morning, dear." Off he went without any
objections. Harry was so understanding. I retired early that night. As I
was lying there, it suddenly struck me. I never gave Philip my address.
He wouldn't know where I lived, as I had invited him to dinner. Well,
maybe it was best he didn't come. Bill wouldn't like it. I hoped he
wouldn't ask Bill for my address. The only thing he knew was my
name, Mrs. Pat Armstrong.

Harry came around the following evening. He said he had a lot
to talk to me about. This was about 8:00 o'clock. He said he had just
come in from his office. He hadn't eaten, so I made him a quick
sandwich. I couldn't understand what all the hurry was about. I
wondered what he had to tell me. He was very cautious how he told
me. "Harry," I said, "you don't have to worry about me. I shall
understand. Please tell me what's on your mind." He looked at me
kind of pitiful. He went on to say the case of his e-girlfriend's
shooting had been brought up again for a hearing.

"Pat, that night she accidentally shot herself, I was with her
early in the evening, as she wanted to talk to me about something very
private between us. I can't tell you what it was. I didn't know she had
a gun. They seem to think I had something to do with her shooting.
The case will be heard within the next few weeks." Harry seemed very

upset. I felt sure Harry was not guilty of anything like shooting someone - he was too kind a person. Well, I thought it could have been accidental. I tried to talk him off it, but he would bring it up whenever he had a chance. This upset me. It was helping me move to decide on marrying Bill. I had had so many 'Bills' in my life, it seemed it was a must this time. I told myself I'd been chasing rainbows far too long. It was time I settled down, just forget the past and live for the future. I once read the following in some book. At that time I was full of trouble and self-pity. It went like this:

> Build for yourself a strong box;
> Fashion each part with care.
> When it is strong as your hand can make it,
> Put all your troubles there.
>
> Tell no one else its contents;
> Never its secrets share.
> When you have dropped in your cares and worries,
> Keep them forever there.
>
> Fasten the strong box securely,
> Then sit on the lid and laugh.

I think that is a good thing to do, as life is too short to worry. Harry seemed to like the idea of the strong box. I told Harry I was sorry but I couldn't help him with this kind of trouble. I hoped everything would come out good for him.

I didn't see him for a few days. I was glad about that. I had been too busy working out how and where would I go from here. I had made up my mind to marry Bill. He needed me. Yes, and I needed him too. Now I had to work out what I would do with all my property. Maybe I would leave everything in the hands of my solicitor. He would take care of everything for me.

I realised I was staking a big step in marrying Bill, as his health seemed to be deteriorating. I had a call from Bill. He said he leg was much better and he was not going to the hospital. I told him I'd call him the following night to tell him when to expect me. He seemed quite happy, although I did not mention my decision regarding our getting married. We talked more about how his leg was. I didn't want to talk too long. "So I'll call you tomorrow, darling."

He replied, "Don't forget I love you." That was my Bill.

I started looking over my clothes. I wouldn't need heavy things for California, so I took a lot of clothes and things I wouldn't need to the thrift store. The manageress was surprised to hear I was leaving the country for good, but I was born in the USA. That was my country. I told her that was where I belonged.

I saw my lawyer and he would take care of all that belonged to me in England. I was getting to feel a great happiness coming over me. I had never felt this way ever before in my life. It was going to be Bill, yes, Bill forever and ever. I just didn't want to see or talk to Harry again, unless it was absolutely necessary. I only hoped he was not guilty as regards his ex-girlfriend's shooting. I thought it was strange that it was to be re-heard.

I worked hard all day around my apartment. I spoke to Mrs. Hanson and told her I would be leaving soon for California. She was very surprised, and she wished me well. I said I would write to her when I was settled down.

It was about 4:00 o'clock; I had just made a cup of tea, and Harry arrived. It was a strange kind of meeting. He seemed to know what I was about to tell him. He sat for an hour just talking about his troubles. I didn't know how I was going to break the news to him, that I was leaving for California in two weeks. Harry looked so pale and drawn. He had put on a lot of years since this case came up again. That was all he could talk about. I was so glad I was going away soon. "Harry, I have got to tell you this. It is going to be hard for both of us to take, but I want you to understand this. I shall always be very fond of you. I have decided to live the rest of my life in California." I didn't say I was getting married; that would be too much of a shock for Harry. "You know, Harry, I was born in the USA. That's my country and that's where I belong." Harry took it better than I thought he would. I guess his mind was more on this case that was due to be heard soon. He asked me when did I expect to leave. I told him it would be in about four weeks time.

"I hope I can see you more often, Pat, before you go. I am going to miss you very much. The thought of you going out of my life is to me a tragedy. Maybe I can come to visit you in California." I didn't reply to that. I just smiled.

I got an unexpected call from Bill to tell me to fly to New York. He would meet me there and we would stay a few days in the Bronx, then drive or fly to Palm Springs. Bill said he was feeling so much better. He sounded wonderful, and said he was living for the time when we would be together forever and ever. I replied, "Me too, darling. Bye for now."

The days went by so quickly I had not seen Harry for a whole week. I was glad about that. I'd be flying off in two days, so maybe I wouldn't need to see him before I left. I'd have to call him to say goodbye. It would be mean of me if I didn't.

I never heard from him until the day before I was leaving. He just called me by chance to ask when I was leaving. When I told him the day after, he was surprised, as I had said it would be four weeks. He still insisted he would take me to the airport. "But my dear, I have already arranged with Mr. and Mrs. Hanson, my tenants upstairs. They were going to meet someone at the airport coming in from the USA. So Harry, you don't have to take me."

"Well, when am I going to see you, Pat? I must before you go."

"I am so busy right now, Harry. You could drop by for a short while, but I must retire early tonight."

Harry arrived about 7:00 o'clock. Gosh, did he look miserable. I did my best to keep him off talking about his ex-girlfriend. I made a cup of tea just to pass time along. It got to be 9:00 o'clock and time for us to say goodbye. "Harry, I want to thank you for all your kindness to me. I shall always remember you, and I'll drop you a line when I get settled down in California." I could see he was taking this very badly. "Don't worry too much about this ex-girlfriend's case. I believe in you, Harry. Do let me know the results of the case."

He gave me the biggest hug and kisses - I shall never forget. It was a sad parting and I shed a few tears. He was gone for good, I guessed. I didn't sleep much that night, but was ready when the Hanson's called me to take me to the airport. I told my lawyer I wanted my apartment left as is, as Bill and I might want to use it one day.

I waved goodbye to the Hansons and off I flew. I had a pleasant flight over. Bill was there to meet me. He looked great. He didn't seem to have any kind of limp at all. He said he was fine.

When we got to his apartment Bess greeted us and said she was happy to see me again.

We stayed at Bill's apartment for three days. He suggested we should fly straight to Las Vegas and get married. I immediately agreed to that. Bill was thrilled with the idea of going to Vegas to be married. He was a minister's son, but that didn't seem to stop him getting married in Vegas. We said goodbye to Bess. She was staying there to look after the apartments. Maybe when we both got settled down we would sell my property and also Bill's and buy in California.

We flew to Vegas and were married at one of the little chapels. Bill ordered beautiful flowers. We stayed at the best hotel in Vegas. We had a suite of rooms overlooking the Strip. The weather was perfect, not too hot for a honeymoon. Bill was his old self again.

We stayed in Vegas four nights and returned to Palm Springs. The apartment was full of flowers. In the driveway was a brand new car just for me to run around in. "Bill, how can I thank you, dear? You are so generous to me."

He replied, "Remember, darling, you belong to me now. What's mine is yours from now on, forever." I was so thankful Bill was feeling so much better. We settled down to a wonderful life together. Philip and his lady friend still came around. They made us a party to celebrate our wedding. It was a grand affair, just about 30 people there. We met some nice couples, and we invited them over for drinks one day. They were not a drinking crowd of people. It seems one drink and that was it. We didn't know Philip had been in the ministry many years ago. He retired because of some disagreement. He was with the Religious Science Church. I had some experience with that church many years ago. I liked the way they lived.

Bill and I used to walk a lot now that his leg was quite strong. We were out walking one Sunday morning and we met a couple who were at our wedding party. They stopped to talk to us and said they had just been to church. I inquired which, and they said, "It's only a small church yet, but it is growing. It is the Silent Unity Church." Well, I remembered I used to listen to the broadcast over the radio for many years. It kept me sane at times. They were lovely people. She remarked, "Why don't you come with us sometime?"

Bill answered before I could. "Yes, we would love to." We became members of the Unity Church, and our love and faith in each other had grown tremendously.

We were living a beautiful life now. Bill because more and more interested in it. We had been married more than a year. Our love seemed to grow stronger as the weeks went by.

I hadn't heard how Harry's case had one on. I'd be interested to know what happened. I got a letter from Mrs. Hanson, my tenant, and she told me the sad story. Harry was in jail doing time for shooting his ex-girlfriend. He claimed it was accidental. They had an argument and she brought out a gun and was pretending to shoot Harry. In the struggle for the gun she was shot and killed. That was Harry's story. But it seemed they proved it to be different. He deliberately shot her. I could hardly believe that, as Harry was such a kind person. His apartment had been locked up since.

I got a letter from my lawyer later to tell me Harry's apartment was empty. All his belongings were confiscated as he would be in jail for at least five years. When I look back, I knew there was something troubling him. I didn't suppose I would ever hear from Harry again. That was a sad ending for me too.

Bill had become more and more interested in the Unity Church, so much so he became a minister to a church in the San Diego district. We had to move there to be near his church. I didn't believe I'd become a minister's wife, but I was enjoying it and working very hard helping Bill. He was very well liked and drew a lot of people to his new church. He was a very dedicated minister. We built a bigger church, over a period of five years.

I was beginning to worry a little about Bill's health. He had been losing weight for the past few months. I begged him to see a doctor. After months, he decided he should. The doctor recommended he should have tests and Bill went into the hospital. He was only going to be in there for a few days, but the tests had shown some kind of blockage, so there had to be an operation immediately. My prayers and also the prayers of his congregation would give him his recovery. I felt strongly about that.

Bill was in the hospital six weeks, just fighting for his life. Every day I could see he was failing. I didn't question God. Why should this happen to Bill? He was a good living man and we both were so happy together. We had had just six years together. Bill was young yet, too young to die, just 62 now. I prayed for Bill like I'd never prayed before. My faith seemed to be failing. His doctor told me it was a matter of time, and he wouldn't last much longer. This really didn't sink into my mind as I thought it was going to be life everlasting with Bill.

I stayed with him as much as I could, but he didn't know me. I was with him when the Lord took him. It was the biggest blow I'd ever experienced in my lifetime, as I truly loved Bill.

Months went by and I just couldn't go to church any more without Bill, so I moved back to Palm Springs to our apartments. I was so lonely. Bur for Philip coming around now and then to cheer me up, I don't know what I would do. Philip was living alone in the same beautiful house. I asked him where Roz was. He told me she had married two years before, and he didn't know where she was. He looked much older now, but still a very handsome grey-haired man in his sixties. Philip was such a blessing to me. He could see I had taken Bill's passing as a hard blow to life.

I decided I would take a trip back to England to see my son and family. I told Philip of my intentions. He immediately suggested he would come with me for company. That I accepted, as I did need a shoulder to lean on right now.

We stayed at my apartment. Everything was just as I had left it six years ago. It had to be cleaned up and Philip helped me. But I just couldn't get Bill off my mind. I didn't think I ever would. How could I spend the rest of my life without him? I told myself that many times.

Philip took me up north to visit my son David and his family. I was a big surprise when my son told me he had just been divorced. I didn't ask any questions, why or what for; that was his business. He was living alone now, as his two children were in college; one was married. I felt so sorry for him I suggested he should come back with us for a holiday. David stayed a couple of weeks and then left for home again as he had a prosperous business to look after.

Philip and I enjoyed this trip to England. We went up to London to shows and dinners. It seemed like old times again for me. There were new tenants in my apartments now. As I was passing Harry's apartment, I just wondered where he was. But I must not inquire; he could be out of jail by now. I just felt I didn't want to be mixed up with Harry's affairs any more.

I thought this was going to be my last visit to England for a long time, or even ever. Philip was helpful to me to decide if I needed these apartments. He came with me to my lawyer and we decided we should sell them. I felt I had no more interest in ever living in England again. All my property and belongings must be sold. I picked out a lot of things I had shipped over to Palm Springs. I gave my son some valuable antiques that Jerry had left me. We had spent a few days sorting things out. Philip and I were ready to fly back to Palm Springs.

We arrived right on time. Philip packed up his car and we drove home. When I opened the door of my apartment, I felt Bill was still there. Everything that belonged to him was still there untouched. It made me feel so sad. The people in the other two apartments came to greet me. I had not met them before. One was a gentleman in his fifties, I presumed, and there was a retired couple in the other apartment. They were very kind to me, but Philip kept a very close watch on me. He came over every day. I found out later that Bill had his apartments up for sale, and his lawyer was looking after all his interests in this matter.

I had to notify Bill's lawyer of his death. He was shocked to hear it. I was fortunate to have had my name in all Bill's property as joint ownership so there were no problems. I was glad the apartments all got sold. I could settle down to live here permanently.

Palm Springs was a bit too hot for me at times, so I bought a house up the coast from Laguna Beach. It overlooked the ocean. Philip was disappointed I was leaving Palm Springs, but I told him I would spend my winters there. And Philip would come to visit me in Laguna. He still wasn't very happy with those arrangements. He was going to miss me far too much.

Chapter Ten.

Philip was helping me to get settled in my new home. I was going to like it much better than Palm Springs; there seemed to be more air here. I had a sister who lived just a few miles from Laguna. I hadn't seen or heard from her for many years. I didn't think she knew I had been living in the USA for the past six years, but we never had anything in common. I thought one day I would try to find her. I didn't know if she was still at the same address or even married to the same man.

Philip would come over every week and sometimes stay overnight. One day we went to do some shopping in Laguna and stopped to have a cup of tea at a very nice motel restaurant on the beach. As we were about to leave, we came into contact with another couple who were just entering. Well, I hardly knew her. It was my sister and her husband. It was a surprise for both of us. "I didn't know you were evening America, never mind California," she remarked. We stood and talked and she invited us over to her place. I said we would see her one day; she gave me a card with her address. It was in San Clemente. I guess she thought Philip was my husband, and I presumed the man she was with was her husband. There were no questions asked at that moment. We said 'bye for now and that was it.

Philip was having ideas of buying a house to be nearer to me. He told me he couldn't be without me for too long. I was feeling the same way about him, but it wasn't that I was in love with Philip. I guess it was because he had been by my side for so long, and was there when I needed him. I think one can grow to love a person who is so kind to you.

Philip had an idea that I was of independent means, and I didn't need him financially. So he knew I wasn't after his money. We had a good understanding of each other's needs in life. We seemed to fit in well. I think marriage was far from our minds.

Philip came up and took me to see a house in Laguna. It was high on a hill. That I didn't like, so we looked at several, and Philip decided on a duplex on the ocean front. He kept his house at Palm Springs for the winter.

Philip moved in and was very happy there, just to be nearer to me. I felt the same way. One day when I was having a walk along the coast I found a seat and sat looking at the ocean. It was just a beautiful coastline. I was so happy to live there.

An elderly gent asked if I minded if he could sit next to me. I replied with a smile, "Why don't you? It's free." He just laughed. Well, people somehow do like to talk, so I let him ramble off. What a story. I was very interested. He had a lot to tell me. Of course he was a widower that had just lost his dear wife of 30 years, and he was terribly lonely. I would guess his age to be about 60 or 65, well preserved and well groomed too. I always looked at a man to see if he was clean and well cared for. And I used to look at their teeth to see if they were clean. Now, I look at their eyes. They seem to tell me more about a person. His eyes were really a bright blue. He sat about an hour just telling me about his past life. He said one time he was a big gambler and had lost a lot of money years ago, but went on to say he had made plenty since he had stopped gambling. He wasn't what I call a blow bag. He wasn't trying to make an impression on me. I think he could see I was a wise person that would listen, and he enjoyed talking to me.

He asked if I walked every day. "No, not every day, but I'd like to. I like company when I am walking."

He agreed with me and suggested we should meet right here. "When you need company I'll be happy to walk with you." I thought that was nice of him, so we arranged to meet twice a week for walks together. I loved walking. I was used to walking in England. I had missed it a lot. besides, it's so good for you.

I got looking forward to seeing Len. Oh yes, he gave me his name as Leonard Jones. I said I was Pat. I didn't give him my surname. When he mentioned his name was Jones, I said that sounded either Welsh or English. "Yes," he said, "my parents were Welsh." I thought that was funny meeting a Welshman so far away from Wales. He did mention my accent when I first met him; how he loved to hear me talk. I get that many times. I shall never lose my accent. I don't want to.

We had some nice walks along the coastline. We always finished up having afternoon tea somewhere. He did enjoy it. We had quite a long walk one afternoon and we eventually came near where he lived. He asked me if I'd like to see his house. Well, I had known Len for about six weeks now, and I knew I could trust him, so we walked along a very nice street not far from the ocean. It was an older type of house but well preserved. We were greeted by his housekeeper, a little grey-haired lady. She was very pleased to meet me, and she asked if I wanted a drink of anything. I told her I only

drink tea in the afternoons and she made tea and home-made cake.
She sure was a lovely lady. Len was honest with her and told her how
he had met me some weeks ago, how we both enjoyed walking.

Philip was busy settling in his new home. I hadn't seen him for
two weeks. He called me to say he was coming to see me the next day,
so I called Len to tell him I wouldn't be seeing him. He sounded
disappointed, "but I'll see you on Thursday."

Philip told me he was pleased with the duplex he had bought.
He didn't like the tenants in his other apartment. They were two men,
so Philip said he would give them notice to leave.

We found Laguna to be a busy place. We weren't used to
crowds like this.

Philip took me over to see his apartment. It had two bedrooms
and two baths, quite a big apartment. I think I preferred my house;
there seemed to be a different type of people here. I thought Philip was
going to have a problem renting his apartment to the kind of people he
would like.

I had to tell Philip about how I met Len. He didn't like the idea
of me meeting Len twice a week for walks. "After all, Pat, you don't
know much about this man. You have to be careful these days."

"Oh, Philip, I am used to meeting people and I am a good
judge of character. Len is a very respectable gentleman. I'd like you to
meet him some day. Then you can judge for yourself."

"Pat, I just don't want to share you with anyone. Forgive me
for being like this. I have got so used to you now being with me, I find
I can't bring myself to think you are seeing some other man. Maybe I
am selfish."

"Philip, if that will make you a happier person, I won't see Len
again."

Weeks went by and I never went to walk with Len. I didn't call
him to tell him why. Instead of walking, Philip was fond of fishing, so
that's what we did much of the time. We sometimes took a boat out
for a day. Philip seemed like he had taken me over in a way I didn't
like. After all, I was not engaged to him. He was to me a very good
friend. I didn't know how Philip considered me to be his intended wife
one day, but he hadn't given me any ideas of such. So why did he try
to advise me what I must do? Philip wasn't like Bill. It seemed Philip
didn't trust me.

I decided I should call Len and have a walk with him
occasionally. Why shouldn't I? I had to tell Len why I hadn't seen him

for a few weeks. He was a very understanding person. "Don't worry, Pat, I can see I'll have to share you with your friend Philip." Len told me he had a son who was married, but lived in Mexico. His wife was a Mexican. They had a prosperous business there. He said he didn't see much of them.

I got a feeling of attachment to Len as time went on. He was a different kind of man than Philip - very relaxed to be with. He wasn't too generous but he always paid his turn when we went out for afternoon tea. I think there was a reason for it, because as I knew him more, he told me his wife was an invalid for five years before she died. He had a very lonely life as his wife was in a mental home. He went on to say he was introduced to some lady and he got to a very close relationship with her. He spent a lot of money on her, bought her a car, rings, etc. He thought one day they would marry, but she just walked out on him for a younger man. So, Len wasn't going to be taken in again. I didn't blame him.

Philip had rented his apartment to one man. He said he was an older man and seemed quite respectable. Philip dropped by to tell me all his news. I thought he seemed a bit unsettled in his mind as regards living in Laguna. He did say he didn't like the crowds. Of course it was summer and one could not find a parking place for one's car, which I think annoyed Philip many times. I didn't think I'd like to marry Philip, period, as he seemed he couldn't settle anywhere for long. It wouldn't surprise me if he went back to Palm Springs to live again.

I was really enjoying living here and the lovely walks along the coast, and I enjoyed Len's company. I didn't think I would return to live in Palm Springs again, even if Philip did. I think Philip got the feeling I was growing closer to Len as the months went by, and I was neglecting him. Maybe he was right.

I was in town one day shopping and I came across a thrift store. I went in inquired what it was for. It was a better class of stores than the others I'd seen, and the lady told me she was the owner. It was a consignment store. I noticed the clothes were in very good condition, could hardly have been work more than once. I had quite a long talk with her. She told me she was a widow, and she opened up this business for something to do. I went back many times to talk with her. I also brought some clothes for her to sell.

After a few weeks of knowing her, she seemed the kind of person I'd like to know more. She came to visit me several times and I went to her lovely apartment not too far from where I lived. One day she asked me if I'd like to go into partnership with her, and we would open up a bigger store. I thought that would be great.

We found a larger store and advertised quite a few times in the local papers. We got some lovely things and good class clothing. I was really enjoying this new adventure. Philip was surprised to hear the news. Also Len - he came in the store nearly every day as it was near where he lived. I liked him to do that. He was good company. I didn't walk with him now. I got enough exercise in the store, and I walked to the store every day. We met a lot of new people here. I just loved the people. I was happy doing this.

My love life had been sadly neglected these past months. No one seemed to want me, only Len. He was the one who would give me all of his love. We hadn't come to that state yet, but I had a feeling we would before long. He seemed to be growing on me, more so than Philip. Len gave out more, and of course he saw me every day now. I looked forward to that. I didn't think Len had the slightest idea of my wealth, so he hadn't asked any questions regarding that. He took me as I was. I realised I didn't need anyone for financial reasons. Money didn't come into it now. I was seeking the real love of a man.

We had been living in Laguna for three years now and Mary, my business partner, and I had got a very prosperous business going. Philip called at the store. I hadn't seen him for two weeks. He seemed to be worried about something. At last, after a lot of persuasion, he told me he had intentions of selling his duplex as he wasn't happy to live in Laguna. He was thinking of buying somewhere in San Clemente. It seemed a quieter place to live. I did agree with him. I liked Laguna but it was too busy a place to live there. It was good for our business.

Philip seemed to have grown away from me since Len came into the picture. I think he realised Len had become a very close person to me, so maybe this was the reason he wanted to move away from me. Philip said he would let me know when he would be moving. I said I'd go with him to San Clemente to look at houses.

We had a good look around at the houses in San Clemente. I saw one or two I thought I'd like. I loved the Spanish type of house they had there. Philip didn't like them; he wanted something more modern.

We spent a day there. I had nearly decided to buy a niece Spanish type of house. Philip couldn't make up his mind. He had two to choose from. One was overlooking the ocean just one block from the beach. The one I liked was near the centre of the town, not too big, just two bedrooms, two baths, just right for me. Philip's house he thought of buying was much bigger. Why he wanted a big house like that I wouldn't know.

So two days later we went back to decide on the houses. I bought the Spanish house and Philip bought the larger house near the ocean. That was all settled.

I remembered I had a sister who lived in San Clemente. I had her card with me, so we called her. She was pleased to hear from me again after all those years of not knowing where I was. She and her husband owned a six-apartment building. They lived in the largest one. It was very nicely furnished. When I introduced Philip to them, they were surprised it was not my husband, just a dear friend; but they accepted that.

We didn't stay long. We told her we had bought two houses here, and we might eventually come to live here, as Laguna was nice but too busy for us. We promised we would see them again in a short period of time. We didn't have much time to tell them all the things that happened to me in the past 10 years. One day I would tell them.

Now I had to decide if I was going to stay in Laguna or move to San Clemente. I had my business to attend to. Philip thought I would sell my share of it and move to San Clemente where it was more peaceful. I told him I would think about it. Len didn't like the idea at all. He was afraid of losing me.

Philip sold his duplex and moved to San Clemente. He was much happier there. I liked my Spanish home, but I had a lot of adjustments and decorating to be done before I could move into it, so it took some weeks before I could live there.

Philip was calling me every day now. Why, I couldn't guess. He seemed to be so much happier in his new home. I was glad he didn't return to Palm Springs to live. I'd miss him too much. I didn't want to lose him altogether. I had known him for many years and he was helpful to me in many ways.

I told Mary, my business partner, I had bought a house in San Clemente. She was surprised as I hadn't been in Laguna for very long. I told her I didn't like the busy part of it. San Clemente was so much quieter. "I think I shall sell my house here and eventually live in San Clemente." Mary was interested in buying my house in Laguna, so after a few days of considering it, she bought it. Now that was no problem for me.

When I told Len, he was really upset about my leaving Laguna. I said I'd be in the store at least three days a week. "You can see me there." That didn't seem to satisfy Len, and he wanted more of me than that. He came in to be with me every day I was there, and helped me by marking things. He was a great help. He did things like that which I knew Philip wouldn't do.

I called my sister to say I would be around later in the day. I was surprised to hear she was in the throes of divorcing her husband. He had left her just two weeks before. She was visiting me a lot now, and Philip got quite friendly with her. I thought Ann was glad to have some company. They were seen out a lot together.

I asked Philip how Ann was. "Oh, she's just a wonderful person." I was kind of glad for him to find more company than mine as Len was taking up much more of my time.

I was glad for both Philip and Ann, although I missed him dropping by. I had not been too happy myself these past weeks. I thought I was getting that old feeling back again to return to London. I missed those people in the pubs there. They were just a joy to be with. Maybe I'd have a trip back there soon.

I got tired of travelling to Laguna nearly every day to the store, so I decided to sell my share of the business. Mary bought me out, so that was no problem. Len was really upset to hear that, as from now on I wouldn't see him unless I invited him over to see me. I felt I didn't want to see anyone just then. I didn't know what had come over me those past months. Maybe I needed a change. I called my sister and I suggested she and I take a trip to England. She had a son there and I'd visit my son. She thought that was a great idea. Before she could change her mind, I met her and we booked our flight for England within three weeks.

Len called me nearly every day and was sad to hear I was going to England. I think he was wondering if I might stay there for good, as I had talked to him about London and how I loved the people there.

My sister's son met us at the airport. He lived just outside London, so we stayed with his family. I went up north to see my son. I hadn't heard from him for about six months, but he was still in the same house. He had remarried a very nice person, much younger than he. He seemed very happy.

When I returned to London I went to see all the places I had been acquainted with many years before. London had not changed one bit, only everything cost more.

I had several trips to the coast that gave me a great thrill. There seemed to be something there that I couldn't find in California. The people were so friendly. I walked along the promenade where I once met Ed with the dog. I seemed to be living it all over again. I had to go to see the people at the pub where I used to work.

One evening I was having a walk and met Jim, one of the men who used to help in the pub when I was there. He was surprised to see me, and asked me if I'd like a drink. He took me into the pub where I used to work. Well, I looked around and meet quite a few people I knew. We had a real get-together. Everyone was asking me, "Are you coming back, Pat? We do miss you." Gosh, I felt like saying yes.

The memories were too much for me to say yes. I was told that Harry was out of jail, but was a very sick man. I was afraid I might meet him. This urge I had for returning to live in England had left me. California, I love you. When I get back there I'll never leave you. I just had a silly urge to pick up people where I had left them 10 years ago. I realised this doesn't work. One can't live on past memories. Oh, those happy memories of Jim and Jerry and dear Molly. I guess I was just chasing rainbows. I had to come down to earth and live a different life when I got back to California. I had to forget little ol' me, and start to think of helping someone else who needed help.

Chapter Eleven.

We had six weeks in England. My sister and I were happy to get back to California. Philip met us at the airport. He gave Ann a big kiss and me just a peck on the cheek. I knew then it was getting serious between those two. I wondered if he really would marry Ann. He was a hard one to catch.

I called Len and he was there to see me within the hour. I was happy to see him again, but it didn't make any impression on me as regards any serious love affair. I often thought how much Bill meant to me.

I'd been back in San Clemente now some weeks. I was shopping one day and met a lady from England. She told me how many times she had returned to England maybe to stay, but couldn't take the weather. I met her several times as she lived only two blocks away from where I lived. I got to know her as Betty. She asked me to join a club called The Daughters of the British Empire. I did and I enjoyed their company. They were born in the U.K., Unighted Kingdom. Some were Scots, some Welsh and Irish. Betty was a Liverpool girl. We had a lot in common.

One day we were out walking. We came across a thrift store that had just opened up some weeks previous. We went in and talked to three of the ladies who were running it. They told us it was to help children. We asked if we could help. They welcomed us with open arms. Betty and I worked two days a week. It was just growing then. We both loved meeting people. This store got too small for all the goods that were coming in, so we took a larger store and had more people working for us. It was just like a happy family. We all worked so hard, and over a period of years we rented the store next door. Now they had two stores.

Betty and I met a lot of people from England. We were known as the two English gals. They used to come in to hear our accents.

I didn't seem to have much time for Len these days, although he called me most every day. I saw Ann and Philip shopping. They looked very happy together, but I couldn't see Philip getting married.

Len and I went around to Ann's apartment several times to play cards. We spent Christmas and New Years with them. There was no sign of marriage between Philip and Ann.

Ann told me we had a cousin on my father's side who lived just outside Los Angeles. She was our cousin Annie. I had heard about her when I lived in England, but never met her. She was married to a Scot from Glasgow. He was a very nice fellow. We all seemed to fit in well, had lots of parties together.

We travelled a lot with Ann and Philip, but I could see there was no sign of those two getting married. Philip seemed to be happy in how things were going for him. Why should he marry? Len and I with Ann and Philip went to Las Vegas for a long weekend. I never entertained Len sleeping with me, and I don't think he expected it. But it was different with Ann and Philip. He seemed to expect that kind of treatment from Ann. That seemed strange to me as Philip had never propositioned me in any way all the time I knew him. Maybe I wasn't his type.

We had a wonderful four days in Vegas. Len was the lucky one. He won a lot of money. He wanted to share it with me, so he took me shopping and bought me a beautiful gold chain with a diamond pendant. I was very surprised he bought me such expensive jewellery, and he got nothing in return for it. This was the first time he had done this - flowers, yes, but not expensive gifts like this. I thought he just wanted to share his winnings with me. I think Len was a very wise person. He never offered me marriage. He knew I was too independent financially. I didn't need any kind of support in that direction. It seems I had grown to omit my sexual part of life. I didn't seem to have met anyone who could arouse my feelings in that way. I had always considered it sacrilegious and didn't understand people who didn't think that way. I didn't think you could buy true love and affection. I did admire Len for a lot of things. He was a very loyal friend. Also he wasn't a woman hunter. I appreciated Len's kindness to me, but there was a blank space between us that couldn't be fulfilled. He wasn't like Bill.

The trip to Vegas didn't do a thing for me. I seemed to be going around in circles. I was not getting out of life the things I really needed. I realised I had to get to know myself better. Sometimes having money to burn can spoil one. I have known the time when I used to buy two cod fish heads for the cat, but I made fish cakes from them for our dinner. I used to think money was the answer to everything. How untrue it is. As one gets more wealthy, it seems one can become a lonely person. I think this had happened to me. When you have nothing, you haven't much to worry about. When you have money, you worry someone might take it from you.

I went back to the thrift store and started to work again.
Betty and I always saw the funny side of things and people. One day
in the store a lady had lost her little four-year-old girl. We couldn't
find her. Then I saw a little girl as I thought to be a girl, and I said,
"Are you Shirley?"

He looked at me in disgust, "No, I am a boy!" You just can't
see the difference at times, and I said out of the blue, "How do you
know you are a boy?"

He quickly answered, "I wear blue shoes." I thought that was a
good answer.

Thinking of children, I remember when all the children were
evacuated during the war. One of these evacuees, a little boy about
seven years old, stood outside the local church one Sunday morning.
The minister was just going into the church and spotted this little boy.
He said to him, "Good morning, son. Are you coming to church? Have
they asked you in?"

"Yes," he replied, "and they have just asked me out." This
could be a true story. Children say the darnedest things.

I kept myself busy at the store. I was enjoying meeting the
people who came there. Len used to come in a lot. He could see I
wasn't my old self. I didn't seem to want to tell anyone how I felt.

I thought I'd better see a doctor. He told me I was on the edge
of a nervous breakdown and I must get away somewhere. I had quite a
long talk with him. He tried to tell me things about myself that I didn't
realise were wrong. He said I was thinking too much about myself,
and I had developed a big problem that really wasn't there at all. I was
surprised he asked me how my love life was. I had to tell him the
truth; I had none going for me just then. He seemed to think that was
my biggest problem. But I said, "What can I do about a physical need
like this?" I had to admit to him I thought I was being neglected as
regards that. He gave me a thorough examination and found nothing
abnormal. He went on to say he thought I needed an absolute change
in my life. "Why don't you take a trip to the islands?"

"Who with?" I said.

"Do you need someone? Why don't you go it alone? Then you
will meet new people." Well, that kind of shocked me for a moment.
They I thought, why not? I felt I wanted to be alone for while. I
thanked him for his advice, and took it.

Chapter Twelve.

I flew to Honolulu and stayed at the best hotel on the island. It was packed with people. I bought some books to read and relaxed on the beach. At 4:00 in the afternoon I would have my usual cup of tea. As I sat there I pushed my book on the floor. I was picking it up and a gentleman caught hold of it before me and handed it to me. I thanked him, and when he heard my accent, that started the conversation with him. He asked if he could join me for a cup of tea. "Please do; I need some company." He was a well-dressed person, and he had that adorable smile that was so fascinating to see. He told me he was from New York but his parents were English and he had lived in London for many years. I asked him the question, "Are you here alone?"

"Yes, I am. My doctor ordered me to do this. I lost my wife 12 month sago. She passed away very suddenly." We didn't dwell on it, as I knew he didn't want to talk about it.

I told him I was alone and that I was taking this trip for the same kind of reason as he was. He said, "My name is Bill Williams, what's yours?"

"I am Pat Armstrong."

"Can I call you Pat?"

"Please do."

When he said Bill Williams, my heart gave an extra beat. I told him I knew a Raymond Williams who lived in Palm Springs, but he didn't know him. Well, I thought, has God sent me another Bill? It looks like it. He looks a very fine man, and quite a charmer. I guessed his aged as about 65, but he told me after he was 60. I was surprised. He was a well preserved man.

Bill was staying at the same hotel as I, so we saw a lot of each other. We enjoyed each other's company. He told me he had no children, and he had been retired from business for the past 10 years. Bill loved to swim every morning, so I joined him. The water was so warm. I was just enjoying having someone with me and to think he was another Bill. It gave me a great thrill. I had only booked in the hotel for seven days. Bill was going to be there for a month or maybe six weeks. He begged me to re-book my room for as long as he would be there. So I just did that. I thought it couldn't matter to anyone how long I'd be away from home. Len - I hardly gave him a thought. I'd been here nearly two weeks and I hadn't written to him yet.

Bill and I had spent three weeks together. He hired a car and took me all over the island. We had a great time. I felt I wanted to hug and kiss him, but we hadn't even got to that state yet. Bill was a reserved kind. He really made me feel so loving towards him. I guessed he would have to make the first move. I thought, when? I didn't intend to rush things. We had a few more weeks to go yet, and he was so much like my Bill, as I remembered him.

We went to a luau dinner show. The dinner was great, but the drink was pure fruit. One drink of it and it really made one happy. I noticed a lot of people didn't drink it. Bill had two drinks and he was a different person. He told me after that he didn't drink any alcohol, but he thought this was just a fruit drink. This fruit drink made him talkative. He told me about himself and his business. He had been in the realty business all his life and he owned property in New York and also a house in Palm Springs where he and his wife used to spend the winters. Bill wasn't boasting about his wealth. He knew I was interested in property as I told him I had just bought in San Clemente. He said he always wanted to live in San Clemente, but his wife preferred Palm Springs.

That night was quite hot; we sat on the beach until midnight. The mood was just coming to the full. It was too beautiful to go to bed. Occasionally Bill would reach over to hold my hand.

We talked on religion. He said he had not any religion, but his wife went to the Unity church. I told him that my late husband was a Unity minister before he passed on. He could talk about the Bible and quoted several sayings from different chapters I didn't know. I had only once tried to read the bible and it was too confusing for me.

It was past 1:00 o'clock and we decided to retire to bed. He took me to my room, which was on the floor above his. He thanked me for a lovely evening. "I am the one to thank you, Bill. I had a wonderful evening." I gave him a peck on the cheek, and he returned it with a big hug, and we parted.

I lay on the bed for a while, just thinking what a grand fellow he was, when there was a knock on my door. I opened it and behold it was Bill. "Pat, I just had to see you again. Can I come in?"

"Yes, Bill, please do. What's the mater? Can't you sleep?" I asked with a smile.

"No, I couldn't get you out of my mind. I had to come to tell you I have fallen in love with you. I hope you don't mind, Pat."

"Bill, darling, I just love the thought of having you near me." We sat and talked and we both got tired so we lay on the bed. He just cuddled me, and I lay there in a dream. This is Bill. He is my Bill. He acts like him.

We both fell asleep and woke up at 6:00 o'clock. We both were fully dressed. We looked at each other and began to laugh. "We are two sleepy people, all right." he said; "too sleepy to make love." But before it was breakfast time that was different.

Bill called for breakfast to be served in his room for two. I thought I was dreaming again. Here I had my Bill again. I hoped he would never leave me. But I reminded myself this was just a holiday affair. Maybe Bill would go home to New York and forget all about me.

These six weeks went by so fast. Bill suggested I would break my journey and get off at New York to be with him for a few days. I thought that was a wonderful idea. Bill had a house in Manhattan and one in Flushing. We went to Manhattan. It was a very old type of house but it was in wonderful condition. It had four bedrooms and two bathrooms, one on each floor. He had a lady housekeeper, but she was away on vacation for two months, so we had the house to ourselves. I loved these older houses. They seemed to have a warm feeling around them.

Bill said, "Make yourself comfortable; it's yours for the asking, Pat." It sounded like he had made up his mind. I had at our first meeting; I knew he was for me.

I stayed one week there, and I now suggested, "Bill, what about coming back to California with me?"

He grabbed my hand and agreed to that. "Pat, I just can't let you out of my life. I'd love to live in California. I always wanted to, but my wife loved New York." Bill packed a lot of things and left a letter for Jane, his housekeeper, to say he had left for California and would call her when he got there.

We had a pleasant flight over. Bill hired a car and we drove to San Clemente. He liked my older house too, so we were agreed on that. I didn't know how long Bill was going to stay, but I didn't ask him. I felt I wanted him to stay forever.

We had been home three days. I thought I should see my sister. I called her, and she wanted to know how I was and what kind of a holiday I'd had. We went over to see her. Philip wasn't there. I asked her how Philip was, and she told me it was finished between them. She hadn't seen him for two weeks. I was surprised to hear that. I knew he was a hard man to catch as regards marriage. I introduced her to Bill as a dear friend of mine. Ann gave me a funny look. I guess she was wondering who and where did I find a good looking fellow like Bill.

We didn't stay too long. I told her I would call her one day. I took Bill up to Laguna. He had never been there before. He said he liked San Clemente far better - seemed more peaceful there.

Bill had been with me three weeks. He did remark several times that he ought to go home. "Pat, I don't want to wear out my welcome."

"You'll never do that, Bill, but I guess you have a lot of business to attend to."

The night before he left we talked until midnight. "Pat, I want a promise from you before I leave." I looked at him; he had a severe look on his face.

"Bill, what do you want from me more than I have given you?"

"All I want, Pat, is a promise of marriage. When can you marry me, darling?"

"When you want me."

Bill said he would go back to New York, get everything settled, return as soon as possible and we would get married. I had never felt so happy since Bill passed on. This Bill would fill my heart with happiness.

I took him to the airport. Bill kept on waving to me until the plane was out of sight. I had a big lump in my throat when he had gone. "Please come back soon, Bill. I can't live without you."

I drove home to an empty house. I could hardly bear the thought of living alone again. Bill called me when he arrived home. I was so happy to hear his voice again. He said he would call again to let me know how everything was going on, as he was going to sell most of his property.

I didn't know if I should call Len again, but he had been so kind to me. I'd better call him. He was glad that I was home again. "When am I going to see you, Pat?" How could I answer that? I told him I was tired and that I would call him again later.

I had been home just two days and Philip called me. He wanted to come around to talk with me. "OK, come tomorrow at 4:00 and we will have tea together." I wondered what he would have to say about my sister Ann. I hadn't heard what happened between them, but I knew Philip better than my sister.

He was around on time for tea. He didn't look very happy. I asked him if I could help him. "No, I don't think so, Pat." I didn't ask him again. I changed the subject. "I hear you have a new boyfriend, Pat. How did you enjoy Honolulu?"

"I just loved it. Bill and I had a fantastic holiday together."

"So it's another Bill," Philip remarked.

"Yes, and he is just like my Bill."

"Is this serious, Pat?"

"I didn't want to tell him it was, so I said, "Maybe, Philip.""

"Well, so he has beaten me to it. Pat, you know I always wanted you."

"I never knew that, Philip. I thought you were a born bachelor. What happened between you and Ann?" I asked.

"Pat, she isn't like you. We just didn't hit it off. In some ways she was so much different from you."

"Philip, you don't expect us to be the same."

"Who is this Bill you have now and where did you meet him?"

"That's a lot of questions to answer, Philip. I met him in Honolulu. He was staying at the same hotel. I intended staying only one week but Bill was going to be there six weeks, so I stayed on to be with him."

I didn't know why Philip had suddenly become interested in my affairs. When I introduced him to Ann he just lost interest in me.

Philip came around to see me nearly every day after. He had told me it was all through with Ann. He was putting me in a funny position with Ann. I didn't want to hurt Ann's feelings. I didn't know if Ann really wanted Philip for marriage. From what Philip told me, she did want to marry him.

Well, I guess I must keep out of this mix-up. I tried to be out when Philip called. I did go back to help in the store for a few days. I heard Len had been in the store looking for me for a couple of weeks. He came in when I was there and was surprised to see me working in the store again. When he saw me, he said, "Hello, Pat; how are you?" but it was a different kind of greeting than he used to give me.

"I am feeling wonderful, Len - never been so happy for a lot of years."

"You were away for six weeks, Pat. I thought you were only going to be away one week."

"Len, it was just so beautiful there. I just couldn't leave."

"When am I going to see you, Pat?"

That was a hard question to answer. "I'll call you, Len." I left him to serve a customer. I made myself busy talking to different people who came into the store.

I didn't call him, as I thought Bill wouldn't like it. I kept having calls from Philip. He was a pain in the neck. I wished Ann would take him back from me.

I got a call from Bill to say he wouldn't be seeing me for a few weeks as he had so many things to clear away. I didn't rush him. I knew he would be back as soon as he could.

I had a call from Ann. She said she had heard from our cousin Annie in Los Angeles asking us to come and see her. She hadn't been in good health for a few years. We were surprised to see how she had lost a lot of weight. I hadn't seen Annie for 20 years.

We hadn't been there long and her husband came home. This was the first time I had met him. He was a likeable fellow. I understand they used to go to a lot of drinking parties.

Just four weeks after that we got a call from Donald, her husband, to say Annie had passed on. We all went to her funeral. It was a distressing time for all. We didn't see much of Donald for a few weeks. I got a call from Ann to say he was coming to visit her.

Months went by. I didn't know Ann was seeing quite a bit of Donald. Then one day I got a visit from both of them. I immediately could see what was their next move. Yes, they were going to be married. Would I stand for Ann? They seemed very happy together. They were married and Don came to live with Ann. He sold his house in L.A. I think it gave Philip a big shock when he heard Ann had married so quickly.

I kept getting calls from Philip. It seems I couldn't just push him off calling me. He would come to the store to see me.

It was now six weeks since I saw Bill. I was feeling I was being neglected by him. Why didn't he call me more often? I didn't know that Bill had a heart condition until I got a call from his housekeeper to say Bill was in the hospital with a heart problem.

I at once flew back to see him. I arrived in time to see him at the hospital. He was in the recovery room. I could just see him for a few minutes. I got a terrific shock when I saw him. He had had a stroke. His face was awful to look at. That wasn't my Bill. I could hardly hold back the tears. I took a lot of weeks before Bill came home.

I stayed with him until he was able to walk. I had been with him 10 weeks. He seemed to be making slow progress. Bill thanked me many times for staying with him. What else could I do? I could see he was going to be an invalid for a long time. Marriage was out of the question just now. Bill kept asking me, "You will marry me, Pat, when I'm better?"

"Yes, darling, I am waiting for you. I know you will soon be better. Then we will go and live in California. The sunshine will make you better."

Weeks went by and Bill was able to walk with a cane. He was so anxious to get married and go to live in California with me. His lawyer was looking after all his interests so that was no problem for Bill.

We went to see his doctor and he was pleased with Bill's condition and told him he could travel to California whenever he felt like it.

The week after, we flew to my home. Bill was just fine. We were married three weeks after returning to California. We had a quiet wedding. We didn't have a honeymoon. That would come later. Philip dropped by to wish me all the happiness in the world. "Pat, you didn't tell me about this happy event." I told him how sick Bill had been, but there were no signs of Bill's stroke now. He had recovered marvellously.

We led a quiet life for many months. Don and Ann visited us often, and Philip just hung on to us as a good friend of the family.

When Bill's property got sold I was amazed at the value it brought him. I didn't ask any questions but I do know it was in the range of $200,000. I understood he sold all but the house he was living in. He said we could use it sometime and he left Jane, his housekeeper, accommodations as long as she wanted to live there.

Bill was feeling just fine. We went to Palm Springs for a few weeks as the weather here was getting cooler. We stayed at Bill's house. It was very cozy, not too big. We went to see my apartments. We had a visit from Philip while we were there as he was living in his house just a few houses away from us. Philip got friendly with some lady who was visiting Palm Springs. She was very much younger than he. They would come around often to see us. She was a card player. I didn't know Bill was, so we enjoyed playing cards with them. Tess,

Philip's lady friend, stayed in Palm Springs much longer than she had contemplated. I was thinking this may be a serious love affair for Philip. I didn't know much about her, only that she was a widow taking a holiday after her husband's death of some weeks before.

Ann and Don came over to stay with us for a few days. They seemed very happy. They were going to take a trip back to England to see Ann's son and his family. I asked Bill if he would like to join them on that trip. We could visit my son. Bill replied with a beautiful smile, "Why not? Let's go." I never thought I would see England again. I had no desire really to go. I knew Bill wanted to go, and he said he wanted to meet my son and his family.

We all were on our way over to England just three weeks after. We had a pleasant flight over, and Ann's son met us at the airport. We all stayed at her son's home for a few days. Then Bill and I left for Scotland.

We hired a car and drove many miles around Scotland. The weather wasn't too bad. My son was happily married and his two children were both married and lived in Spain most of the time, so we didn't see them. Bill loved Scotland. We took the train back to London and we decided to go to the coast where I used to live.

We booked in at a very nice hotel on the front. This brought back many memories to me. We were walking along the promenade and stopped to look at the ocean. The water was so blue. We sat there for a while enjoying the ocean view. A gentleman came to sit next to Bill and started to talk to him. I didn't take much notice of him. He sounded like an educated man, but was poorly dressed. His hair was white and he was quite think in his body. I looked at him again and again. My God no, it isn't Harry! Yes, it was! He had been telling Bill a sad story. Harry just didn't recognise me at all. I was glad of that. We just moved along as I didn't want to talk to him. I didn't tell Bill that I knew him. Now that Harry didn't seem to know me I wasn't going to make myself known to him, but he was a changed man. He looked like he was living in a world of his own. Bill remarked to me, "That poor fellow was a very sick man. He didn't seem to know what he was saying." I was glad Harry didn't know me. It would have been a shock to him.

Bill had hired a car so we travelled along the coast to many different towns. It is a beautiful coastline. Bill was just loving it, but he did say he wouldn't like to live there. It was too cold for him.

We went back to see Ann and Donald and spent a few days in London before we flew back home. I realised there is only one London in the world. The Americans love London.

We all got home to San Clemente feeling a little tired, but so glad to be back. Bill looked a little pale. I hoped he hadn't overdone this strength. We rested the next few days.

We had a call from Philip to say Tess and he were in San Clemente and could they come around for cards that evening. Bill was willing, so we talked about our trip to England and had a pleasant evening with them. Tess was a very lovely person. She seemed to be like me in her thinking. She told me she was not about to marry yet, but Philip had suggested marriage to her. I was surprised to hear that, as Philip was not the marrying type. If he could get his love life free, he wouldn't marry. I understood she didn't need anyone financially, as she had been left very comfortably off when her husband died. I thought she was a wise person.

It was my birthday soon. Bill would give me a party, but not at our house. We took the folks out for dinner and champagne. There were about 20 people. Bill had put a small gift box beside my plate. When I opened it, it really took my breath away to see a ten-stone diamond ring. It was something I'd never had before; not that I couldn't afford to buy one like it, but that's a lot of money to spend on oneself. "Bill, I thank you with all my heart." With tears in my eyes I gave him a big hug.

We had a nice evening. Tess and Philip and Ann and Donald came home with us for the rest of the evening. I noticed Bill seemed unusually tired and pale. "Are you alright, Bill?"

"Yes, but I am a little tired."

"Why don't you lie on the bed for a while? As he walked to the bedroom he fell. I just couldn't lift him. I phoned Philip. He came around and helped me to get Bill onto the bed. I called the ambulance. They took him to the hospital.

Bill had another stroke and would be in the hospital for a few weeks. I felt so desperate I just couldn't think. What would I do without Bill?

Bill had to stay in the hospital for several weeks. He couldn't walk a stride. Philip was very helpful. He was always there when I needed him. When Bill came home from the hospital he was in a wheelchair. I had to have the house made so there were no steps for him. The doctor told me he would never walk again. This came as a terrific blow to me. Would I have Bill like this forever? It was a frightening thought. I didn't think I could take it.

As the weeks went by he didn't seem to be getting any better. He wasn't eating like he used to, and he was losing weight. I took him back to the hospital for x-rays and tests. The results were not good. I talked to his doctor. I wanted to know the truth about Bill's illness, but I now wish I hadn't wished for the truth. It hurt me too much. Bill had three months to live. I just couldn't believe it. He was a strong, healthy man when I met him three years before. How could this happen? I didn't tell anyone the results of the tests. I couldn't bring myself to talk about it, and I knew Bill didn't know. He must not know, or it would shorten his life.

I seemed to be questioning God again. Why does this happen to me? When I am happily married something comes along to part us.

I could see Bill was failing pretty fast these past few days. He was in bed all the time now. I had a nurse in to help me. Bill passed on just six weeks after his tests. I was absolutely heartsick. This was the end of any romance in the future. I just couldn't take any more of this losing my lovers. I swore I'd never love again, no, never.

Philip and Tess were so kind to me. I couldn't believe I was alone again. Bill was such a handsome, strong looking man. I sometimes blame myself for taking him to England. It might have been too much for him.

I learned a lot about Bill's financial position after he died. I was very surprised when I heard he had been a terrific gambler and had lost thousands over a period of years previous to my meeting him. His property had to be sold to clear his gambling debts.

Chapter Thirteen.

I had to settle down to a lonesome life once more. I met a lady while shopping. She told me she did voluntary work at the local hospital. She asked me to join. I found it very satisfying to be able to help people who couldn't help themselves, but that didn't seem to fulfil the empty space I had for Bill.

Coming from the hospital I saw Len. He had been in the hospital for a week with some kind of illness that needed x-rays. I didn't ask him what, as he looked very well. He had heard of Bill's passing and expressed his feelings and was sorry to hear it. Two days after, he called me to see if he could come over for a little while. I welcomed the idea as I'd been so lonely these past months. In England I had the people in pubs to talk to, but here it was so much different. The bars here weren't very nice placed to work. I missed England for that. I never was lonely when I worked there. It kind of flashed across my mind, should I return to England and live there again? I had felt so confused these past months.

I talked to Len about it and he begged me not to even think of going back to England to live. "You know, Pat, you wouldn't be happy there for long."

"But Len, there isn't anything to do here. I want to meet people. I love people and I want to be around them. The hospital isn't much of a help to me. I don't like to be amongst a lot of sick people. I may go back again for a few months to see if I really want to live there. It would give me a break."

Philip and Tess dropped by for a while and I told them how I felt about returning to England again. They really were surprised and asked me why this sudden talk of returning to England. "I thought you'd had enough of England."

"Yes, I thought so too, but I am feeling so lonely these days. I expect that's what has made me think of all those people I used to meet in the hotel."

Philip said, "You don't have to be lonely. You have Tess and me to see and talk to."

"But that doesn't answer my needs. I have to have someone to love and to be loved." That was a funny thing for me to say to Philip, as he was always very fond of me.

They were kind to me the following weeks to help me get over this depression. Ann and Donald were very helpful too. But I didn't get any satisfaction from their visits.

I decided to go to England to see my son and tell him my troubles. I stayed with him two weeks and then I went to London and the south coast. I really enjoyed being there. I called Jim. He was one of the waiters at the pub when I worked there. He was surprised to hear I was back in England so soon. He told me he was working in a very nice large hotel in a little town higher up the coast. He said Hastings. I knew it very well. "Come up, Pat, and see me tonight."

"I'll be there." I talked to a lot of people. It was good to be amongst them again. Jim introduced me to the manager. He was a fellow in his fifties. He said in a joke, "Would you like to take a job here, Pat?"

"Gosh," I quickly replied, "I'd love to."

"You've got it. Start tomorrow night."

Well, first I had to find somewhere to live. "You don't need to, Pat. You can live in here."

The day after, I moved into the hotel. This was a very high class hotel, much nicer than the other one I had worked for. The manager was very nice to me. I had to call him Tom. He was Mr. Tom Dawson. His wife was a charming lady. I got on well with her. We seemed to fit in beautifully. I was enjoying all the nice people. They all got to know me as Pat. It seemed like old times again.

I met a few people I had known many years ago. They too were much older. I guess I looked different to them. I may be older but I had never felt younger and happier for a long time. I suppose this was a substitute for Bill. I felt no-one could take Bill's place. This hotel did a lot of lunches and dinner parties. It was a very popular hotel.

I went to see my tenant Mrs. Hanson, but she had left and they had sold the hotel I used to work for. I spoke to a gentleman who lived in their apartment. He told me that Mrs. Hanson had died. It was a sad story. I was sorry to hear it. Mr. Hanson was now living higher up the coast near Hastings. I remembered them so well as a beautiful couple. I was sorry to hear this sad ending of Mrs. Hanson. I mentioned this to a gentleman who used to own these apartments. Yes, he said, it was a sad affair, but didn't say what happened to Mrs. Hanson. "Oh," he said, "aren't you Mrs. Armstrong, or Pat, they called you?"

"Yes, that's right. How do you know?"

"Now, Mrs. Hanson used to tell me about you. I understood you had gone to live in California."

"Yes, I have a house there but I got homesick for England and all these nice people here in the hotels. So I returned just to prove if I really needed to live here again. I don't think I could ever stay here forever. Maybe I'll return to California when the weather gets unbearable for me. I guess if England had lots of sunshine like California I would not have left."

I just kept coming back to London. It had a terrific attraction for me.

"Where did you say you are living now, Mrs. Armstrong?"

"Oh, at the moment I am living in at a nice hotel in Hastings." He looked surprised.

"Why do you have to work, Mrs. Armstrong?" I thought you were an independent lady."

"Yes," I replied, "I am, but I love people and the hotel work. I lost my dear husband in California so I just had to get away to be amongst these nice people again."

"Some day I'll come to see you," he remarked.

"OK, do that. I'll be glad to see you again."

I had been working here for six weeks and had met some very fine men who offered to help me settle here. I had not accepted their offers of dinners or drives yet. I was going to be more cautious now. I was not going to fall for any man. I'd had enough experience. I realised marriage was a very serious step to take. I'd had three marriages up to now. I expected to marry again one day, but for now it was going to be a lover. Yes, I needed lots of loving. There was a very fine looking gentleman who came into the hotel every night. He didn't drink much. He told me he came in just to see me and have a chat. He wanted to take me out for dinner and theatre in London. I loved London; it was part of me.

On my night off I decided to take a chance with this gentleman. He seemed a little younger than I. He told me his name was James William Holden, and said some people called him Jim and most of all it was Bill. "So, Pat, I don't mind which name you call me." How could I have another Bill? I had to call him Jim, so it was always Jim.

We had a very pleasant evening together. He told me quite a bit about his pat life; the usual divorce; it was five years ago and since then he had not dated anyone.

Jim sounded like a busy man; he was a member of a local church and he told me he did a lot of welfare work. He didn't tell me his private business. I thought he was a retired man. Jim appealed to me. I liked his manner. He wasn't like the average man. He didn't even hold my hand all the evening, nor ask for a kiss goodnight.

We got back to the hotel before it closed. He came in for a short period. When the pub closed he had to leave. I thanked him for a lovely evening and that was that. He left me with, "I'll see you tomorrow night, Pat."

"OK, Jim." I nearly called him Bill.

I had a shower and tried to relax, but I kept thinking about Jim. I just could not figure him out some way. I usually can tell the kind of person they are within a short period of time, but Jim had got me guessing.

I seemed to be over cautious about men now. Maybe I should not worry too much regards Jim. He seemed a real gentleman.

I had plenty of mail from the USA. They all were asking, "When are you coming back?" They were surprised by my previous letter that I had settled down here and was very happy doing what I always wanted to do.

We had a big wedding party at the hotel, about 200 guests. Some of them took too much champagne. The men folks seemed to be making love to all the ladies, including me. One fellow really propositioned me. He wouldn't take no for an answer, but I was used to dealing with folks like him. When the drinks are in them they are different people. When tomorrow comes, he won't remember half of what he did or said to me. They usually come in the hotel the day after to apologise for their behaviour.

This fellow did just that. He was very upset and guilty of the things he had said to me the previous evening, and he hoped he hadn't offended me. "Not at all," I replied. I was used to this. I knew how to deal with people who got drunk. After all the apologies from him he asked me for a date for dinner out. I thanked him and gave him a funny look and said maybe one day. I didn't think he liked my answer to his date.

This fellow came into the hotel every night. He would stand beside Jim. I think they had something in common. I never got to know his name. He was a fellow in his fifties, grey hair, but well groomed. That I did notice. I reckon when a men looks clean he must be clean in his ways of living, but one can be fooled.

Strange enough, Jim left the pub early that evening so I managed to talk to this gentleman who was asking me for a date. He did try again to date me, but I didn't answer him. He talked a lot about himself and said he was a free man and had lots of time on his hands. He remarked that he went to the races a lot and would I be interested to go with him to Ascot races the following week. This I'd love to, but I did not promise him yet. "Don't worry, Pat, I am a single man. My name is Fred Wilson. My wife died 10 years ago, and I've been looking for the same kind of lady to Marry." Well, I took a change and said I would go to the races with him. He picked me up - had a Rolls - it looked new. The weather was good, but we didn't back any winners. But it did bring back some happy memories of the past.

After the races were over we took a ride around London and had dinner at a very nice hotel. London always gave me a feeling of home.

Fred proved to be a real gentleman. We got back to the hotel just as they were closing, so Fred didn't come in. I was feeling so happy. I thanked him for wonderful day out. I did mention it had brought back a few happy memories for me. I hadn't told him about my past life. I thought it best not to as yet.

Fred made a good impression with me. He had a few of Bill's ways with him. I could have made love with him, but that was too soon. He just said, "Good night Pat, dear, let's do this again soon."

I foolishly replied, "When, Fred?" That was funny for me to ask him for another date, but I just wanted to see him again.

He immediately said, "Next week, Pat."

"OK, that's a date," I replied. I decided I would take an apartment near the hotel and do just part time work. Two nights a week would be enough for me. I didn't have to work at all, but I enjoyed the company.

I was enjoying my new home. It was great to have my own house again. Fred phoned me every day and dropped around for a cup of tea about 4:00 o'clock every day I was home. He seemed to have a lot of time on his hands.

Fred took me for a drive up the coast. It was a beautiful day. The ocean was so blue and calm. I got a happy feeling to be with Fred, but he sure was a slow worker. I did admire him for that. He didn't realised I was a love-starved gal.

I would be happy to live here forever if we had California weather. We have a beautiful country and coastlines.

We pulled up to a little whitewashed farm house for eats. It had a sign hanging outside that said "Home Made Bread and Cakes." My goodness, the meal was just delicious. We had home cured ham, fresh farm eggs, hot bread, English muffins and some currant cakes. Oh yes, and home made jams. They had set the table with an old lace cloth and service to match, all hand made.

This to me was home again. She was a maiden lady in her sixties. She and her mother lived there alone. They had a man to do outside work. It was spotlessly clean. She told me she fed the chickens and milked the cows every day, hail, rain or snow. She had pigs to feed too. She gave me some sausages she had made that morning. We went down into their cellar. She had every kind of bottled fruit, jams, vegetables, and meat hung up. She had a walk-in refrigerator. I nearly caught my head on a side of a pig. I guess they had to prepare for winter.

She was a beautiful lady - no makeup on and not a wrinkle on her face. I asked her what she used for face cream. She smiled at me and said, "Nothing, only I always wash in rain water." She had an amazing complexion. One doesn't meet people like this often. Her mother, she told me, was 90 years old. Gosh, she looked about 60, such a beautiful, happy person. They do have to work many hours a day in that business. It seemed it kept them young and healthy. There was no doctor within 20 miles of their hotel, so they had to keep well. They had lived that life since they were born, but I couldn't take it. I must remember this about the rain water, though.

Fred and I took a walk up a country road. Everything was so peaceful. The grass was green and flowers seemed to shout 'Hello' to us as we walked along this winding lane. We came to a gate that led to an open field. Fred said, "Let's go through." We walked to the top of a hill. What a view we had! The daffodils were blooming. I got a nearer-to-God feeling as we walked along. Fred took hold of my hand and gave it a squeeze now and then to make sure I was there with him. I had not noticed this before in Fred's attitude. We decided to sit on the grass. It was too warm to walk any further up the hill. We sat there enjoying the warm sun. I didn't seem to have any problems. Fred was near me; that was all that mattered to me. All my problems had blown away with the wind.

Fred did confess to me that he had had many problems in the past few years. I didn't press him to tell me. He mentioned the first year after his wife died he did have a love affair with a younger woman and he was too generous towards her. She practically made him bankrupt. All she wanted was his wealth. He was fortunate to get rid of her. Maybe this was shy he was a slow worker.

He changed the subject and said, "Pat, you look so happy today. I hope I have helped you."

"Fred, dear, you sure have added to my happiness today. I thank you a million."

I was still trying to know Fred. He was a hard man to get to know, but I was enjoying this. There was something about him that intrigued me. We seemed to be people who were happy with the small things in life. He wasn't the same man that I knew at our first meeting.

Fred had too much to drink that night when he propositioned me. There seemed to be two sides to Fred. I couldn't reckon him up yet. I don't remember having had three dates with a man and up to now not even a kiss goodnight. He did put his arm around me to help me up the hill we were climbing. He had plenty of opportunities to take advantage of the situation, but he still remained a gentleman.

I got a phone call from Jim when we arrived home. I couldn't talk to him for long as Fred was sitting close by me. I told Jim I would see him in the hotel the night after. Jim would repeat he had missed me and where had I been these past few days. Now that I didn't live in the hotel, I only worked two nights a week. Jim didn't know I had my own apartment now or I guess he would have come round to visit me.

Fred didn't stay late. We had a cup of tea. He did tell me a little about his interests in football - not the actual game, but he was in partnership with a large "Football Coupons." I remembered the company. I used to send in my coupons every week on the footballs. These people were millionaires a few times over. He went on to tell me it was a family business. He didn't do much work in it. I guess it was run in a big way. He let others do the work. It had taken him many weeks to tell me all this. I was surprised he was so wealthy and seemed happy with the small things in life. I understood Fred had a flat just outside London.

Fred went on to say his grandfather started this business and how it had grown to be the largest Football Coupons in the world. They had horse and dog betting. They were what they call here "bookies." I remember I would send these coupons in every Friday night and hope for a big win. It never came my way. This was the only hope I had to become rich quick.

Fred told me he had a house in Spain and would I go with him for a long weekend. Well, I thought, here we go again: "Good girls never get to Spain." So what? I do consider I am a good person in a way. I think to be.

I didn't think Fred was expecting me to give my body and soul to him on this long weekend. So I accepted his offer for what I hoped would be a wonderful weekend. I needed this. So whatever happens to me, I can take it. I'll trust Fred for a lovely weekend. The weather was good now. "Pat, what about it?"

"I'll be with you, Fred, when you are ready to go. Next weekend sounds great for me."

Fred was ready to leave after I had promised him this wonderful weekend in Spain. I gave him a peck on the cheek and thanked him for his generosity. "Good night, Pat dear." But he didn't return the kiss I had given him on the cheek. "I'll see you tomorrow, Pat.

I saw Jim in the hotel the night after. He was kind of cool with me, but kept asking me questions I didn't want to answer. I just put him off. He could see I didn't like him asking me where I had been the past days. He had no claims on me. Why should he be so demanding as to where I had been? This was not my idea of a friend. He told me he had two tickets for a show in London. Would I like to accompany him on Saturday evening? We could have dinner before the show. Of course this was in London. That was kind of a sudden invitation. I couldn't think how to answer him. I didn't want to offend Fred by accepting Jim's invitation. I said I would let him know later in the evening.

I didn't know anything about Jim's financial position, but I realised Fred was something to be hoped for financially. I had always admired a rich man; they attracted me. How could I tell Jim I was going to Spain with Fred for a long weekend, this weekend? I thought he may judge me wrong. I didn't make a practice of these happy weekends with a stranger like Fred. I shouldn't call Fred a stranger; I seemed to know him as a friend now.

I suddenly thought of a good excuse to refuse Jim's offer of dinner out. I told him my son and his family were coming to stay with me for a couple of weeks. Jim gave me a funny look. He knew it was not true, only an excuse. He seemed taken aback by my refusal. This was the first time I had refused Jim. I was sorry I had to do this to Jim, but I couldn't say no to Fred as regards a long weekend in Spain.

Besides, I had never been to Spain. I needed this romantic weekend, and lots of loving.

I was looking forward to seeing Fred's house in Spain. Fred picked me up in his Rolls and we flew off to Spain. I got that old feeling of happiness I knew Fred could give me.

When we arrived in Spain there was a car and a chauffer waiting for us. We drove along the coast for about 10 miles till we came to a small village. We came to what I would call a small castle type of house, but as we entered I could see it wasn't a small house. The maid showed me my room. The man who took our luggage must have been the butler, I presumed. I was introduced to the housekeeper. She was a Mexican but spoke good English, a lady in her fifties.

Well, this was really something, but Fred and I would never be alone in this house. I noticed my bed was huge, too big for one person. By this time my thoughts were really running away with some funny ideas. Who's kidding whom? - I thought.

There was a lovely meal waiting for us. After dinner we went swimming. It was a beautiful warm evening. We sat on the beach until 10:30. Fred looked a fine healthy he-man. I looked at his body; it was mostly brown. I guess he spent a lot of time here on the beach. Fred surely had a beautiful body, not much hair around. I was glad for that.

As we returned to the house we were greeted by Marie, the housekeeper. She had baked some nice cookies for us. We could have tea, coffee or wine. I chose tea. Fred had a glass of wine with his cookies. I was hoping it would not change his personality. I loved him as he was. I didn't want him to change. He was a beautiful person just now. I kind of thought of the first time I met him. He was quite a sexual man, but the wine was talking for him. I wanted to keep the evening free from wine.

We retired to bed about midnight. Fred took me to my bedroom and reminded me if there was anything I needed to just push the bell and the maid would help me. I thought, which bell do I push if I want Fred any time? "Good night and God bless, dear. Sleep well." Just a peck on the cheek and he was gone. Well, this is something different for me. Maybe we could have found something in common, who knows? I could not relax. I lay there awake for it seemed like hours, thinking and thinking what next could happen to me.

I showered again. I thought that might help me to sleep. The last time I looked at my watch it was 3:00 a.m. I must have fallen asleep after that. I woke up at 7:30. I pushed the bell and within minutes Marie was there. She ran my bath water for me, and perfume to go with it. She put out on the bed a beautiful gown. It was a pretty blue, nearly transparent. I took my time and went down for breakfast in this beautiful gown. I had to admit it was kind of sexy.

Fred was already seated at the table waiting for me. "Good morning, Pat darling. Did you sleep well?"

I had to say, "Yes, dear, I did." I nearly said, "I did miss you, Fred," but I thought I wouldn't sound too eager for what-have-you, Fred. He did say it was a gay long weekend. This word gay can mean many different things. I'd better keep my thoughts clean.

After breakfast we walked along the beach. It was beautiful. We sat down to rest after a long walk. Fred tried to get me talking about my past life. I had to tell him I had three marriages, one was annulled and two of my husbands had died - one in a car accident. I also told him I had a house in California. His eyes really lit up when I told him that. He said he had never been to California but always promised himself he would go there. "Fred, I will give you an invitation one day if I return on a visit. Just now I don't want to live there, although the weather is perfect, just like Spain."

We spent most of our time in the ocean and walking. We had four relaxing nights and days at Fred's house. There was no love making. I felt I was being cheated for some reason. I couldn't understand as Fred was a fine looking, healthy man. Maybe he was waiting for me to make the first move toward this love making.

Fred suggested we fly to Paris for a show. I thought that was a wonderful idea of his. Maybe that would put the icing on the cake for me. He had not shown much affection yet. . Maybe he was on his best behaviour whilst he stayed where his staff was. Paris, in a nice hotel, and he might prove to be a different man. Paris and the shows had got to be romantic for both of us, and could change our moods.

We stayed two nights in Paris. I was surprised at Fred's attitude towards me. He was more relaxed that I had ever seen him.

The first night we were both feeling kind of tired. We had been to a midnight show. By the time we got to the hotel it was 2:00 a.m. We sat on my bed for at least half an hour having a cup of tea. We both got to yawning, so Fred politely said, "Darling, we both are tired. I think we should retire to bed." With a hug and kiss he was gone. Well, this was the strangest long weekend of no love making I had ever come across. I didn't get that strong feeling for making love to Fred. We seemed to have so much in common in other directions. I had a brotherly love for him. This was one of those kinds of loves that would grow slowly but surely. I had to be patient with Fred. I knew one day he would prove his manhood to me. I felt I shouldn't push him into something he was not ready for. The second night was a repeat of the first. I guess I had to play a waiting game.

We flew back to London and stayed one night before he took me home. We seemed to have grown inseparable, but where do we go from here? I was hoping Fred would ask me to marry him. He surely was a slow worker. He left my apartment about 10:00 o'clock. He did give me a more passionate kiss as he said, "Good night, darling. I love you." I thanked him for wonderful time and returned the kisses. He left me in a state of perplexity. I sat up till the early hours of the morning, just trying to work things out. Does or doesn't he really love me enough to want to marry me? I could see I had to prove my love for Fred in a different way than I thought. I had got to the stage I just could not live without him and yet we hadn't proved our sexual demands for each other. If I didn't get any true intentions from Fred soon I guess I'd get the urge to return to California. I could not stay here and not be married to Fred; it would break my heart.

I wondered if his family would be against him marrying a barmaid. Maybe that was delaying him asking me to marry him. I went to work the following evening. Fred didn't come in as usual. I hadn't seen or heard from him for two day; it seemed like a lifetime.

Jim came in. He was happy to see I was back in the hotel again. This was the only way Jim could see me. I had not invited him to my apartment and I didn't intend to. I didn't seem to have any affection for Jim those days. Fred had taken over my life.

I still had not had a phone call from Fred. Why, I wondered. I was counting the hours since I had seen him. I couldn't take the suspense much longer. . Shall I call him? It's three days now. I did phone him and a lady's voice answered the phone. I asked to speak to Fred. She said, "You mean Mr. Wilson?"

"Yes, yes" I said with caution.

"He isn't here just now. He had a car accident a few days ago and he is in the hospital; he is in a coma. No one can see him." My heart sank in my shoes. "With whom am I speaking?" she inquired.

"Oh, just a friend. I am Pat."

"I have heard of you. I am Mr. Wilson's housekeeper. If you call again later I will tell you when Mr. Wilson has come out of his coma."

"But please, can you tell me which hospital Mr. Wilson is in?"

"No, it's no use, Pat, you can't see him. Give me your phone number and I will call you when there is any change in his condition." I just thanked her. My whole world had fallen apart again. I had prayers for his recover. Dear God, help him. I love Fred truly. Do spare him just for me.

It was nearly six days and I had not heard from Fred's housekeeper. I could only presume Fred was in the same condition. The hotel had helped me with this anxiety. Also Jim had come into the hotel to console me. He knew I was very fond of Fred. It was now two weeks. I couldn't wait any longer to hear from Fred's housekeeper, so I called her. There was no change in Fred's condition. It seemed Fred's care was hit by a drunk driver, who was killed. It happened the night Fred had brought me home from our visit to Paris and London. I felt I was to blame for this accident. If he hadn't brought me home, this wouldn't have happened. I was feeling a bit guilty now. I hoped Fred would forgive me.

This had given me a very unsettled feeling. Here I found the man I wanted to marry and he was being taken away from me through this drunken driver.

Jim was a blessing to me. He called me every day. He asked if he could come and see me. I was glad to have him come around. I made him a nice meal together, but he didn't talk much about Fred. I never did know much about Jim's life. I knew he was a member of a church. I asked him to have prayers said for Fred. I didn't know how long Fred would be in this coma; who knows? It could be a long time. If I could only see him I'd feel better.

I worked at the hotel more nights to keep my mind off worrying about Fred. They needed my help just then. We had a lot of parties coming up, the usual weddings. But this one was a celebration of 25 years of marriage. I didn't have much interest in this party, but I tried to be sociable. There were many men there that had too many drinks. They get difficult to deal with sometimes. I had many invitations to an evening out. These didn't count. The day after they don't remember. I think most of these offers were sympathy offers as they knew Fred was sick.

It was now six months since I had seen Fred, and he was still in a coma. I felt this was the end of my relations with Fred. I decided I should accept an invitation from a fellow I knew who came in the hotel pretty often. He knew I was a dear friend of Fred's. His name was Reg. I only knew him as Reg. He wasn't the type who got drunk. We had a nice evening together, which helped me to try to forget Fred. We had several nights out together and he was always a perfect gentleman. He made a habit of dropping in my apartment to have a cup of tea with me. No sign of any love making - he was just a good friend to me. I did appreciate his company. He had helped me over my worries about Fred.

Between Jim and Reg I had lots of company. They were a blessing to me at this time. I was glad of Reg's company the evening I got a phone call from Fred's housekeeper to tell me the sad news of Fred's passing on that very evening. The doctors said had he lived he would have been a vegetable. What a blessing, I thought. I was glad Reg was with me. I couldn't hep but weep. I felt my life was hanging. I could not believe Fred had gone out of my life forever. Reg was very kind to me and I was glad of his company. He was more of an understanding person than Jim. We seemed to knew each other's thoughts.

I didn't know a lot about Reg's private affairs. I only knew he was retired from a government job. I presumed he must have a good pension. He also owned some apartments in Hastings. I had not asked him if he had any family. He did say his wife had died two years before, so I didn't have that on my conscience. He was a single man and as free as the air.

I got a letter from Ann and Don to say they were expecting a visit from Don's brother the next month. "What about a trip over here, Pat? We have talked about you over the phone and he wants to meet you. His name is Allan Garnel. He is a Scot. I think I told you, Pat, his wife died a year ago. He is living in Derby, Connecticut just now. Allan has just returned from the US Navy. His rank was Captain." Ann was very keen on my meeting this fellow, although I didn't feel in the mood for any new acquaintances. No new lovers just yet. I still had Fred on my mind.

I told Ann I couldn't think of a visit to California just then. I had lost a very dear lover of mine. We had intended to marry soon, but he had a car accident and had died. I loved him more than I could say. I also got a letter from Philip and Tess. They were asking when I was going to return to California. I told them I couldn't say when I would visit California again as I had too much on my mind just then. Maybe later in the year as time went by I would decide to make a visit to California.

Ann and Don were disappointed I was not making that trip for some months yet. I told them it would be difficult for me to leave here just then. I didn't go into any causes as to why I could not make that trip. They didn't ask why. I left it an open book for them to guess the reason why.

The weeks were passing kind of fast then. It had been six weeks since my lover had died. I was glad I had the hotel to work for. These people had been so kind to me since Fred died. I had many offers of dinners out, etc. Yes, Reg even asked me if I'd like to take a holiday with him. "What about it, Pat?" That was a quick invitation.

"I'd have to think about it, Reg."

"Where do you want to go, Pat?" I couldn't think of anywhere I would like to go.

Reg was very kind and patient with me. I wasn't in any mood for a holiday with anyone just then. I was enjoying doing my job at the hotel. I worked tow nights a week. It helped me in my thought world.

Jim was a darling, too. He knew Reg came round to see me. They knew each other and seemed to understand my position. I didn't want to offend either of these two wonderful men. I needed their help. There was no love attached to their friendship.

I had started to take long walks along the beach. I seemed to be enjoying the closeness to the ocean, to watch the tide drift in and out. It gave me a calm feeling. I walked most every day. It was very early one morning, I was having a swim and I saw what I thought was just someone having fun in the sea. Then I heard these cries for help. Well, I thought, I can swim but I have never been a lifesaver. They were coming closer to me.

I managed to hold him up until a lifesaver came to our rescue. This was a very exciting thing for me to do. I had difficulty in holding him up as he was a man I think in his fifties and well built. When we got him to the beach, he said he had cramps in his legs. Now he was alright. This does happen with a swimmer. He thanked me several times and said, "Dear lady, you saved my life. I'd like to repay you for this. Can I take you out for dinner sometime?" He begged for my phone number. He said his name was Peter Townley and he was a bachelor. Well, that sounded good enough for me, so I gave him my phone number. Many weeks had gone by and I had not heard from this Peter, so I presumed he was not interested in me.

My walks along the beach became very unusual. I had met so many different people, yes, and lots of dogs that I loved to throw stones for. I had talked to a lot of people who seemed to have many problems and I was a good listener. I loved people, young or old. The older people seemed to attract me more.

One day I was walking along the beach feeling pretty low myself. I still missed Fred; he was my true lover. I noticed what looked like garbage that had washed up. As I got closer to it, I saw it move. To my surprise it was a human being, yes, a lady. She looked to be in her sixties. She was wet through. I asked her if I could help her. She said, "No, I don't want any help. I just want to die." This really gave me a big hurt.

I told her, "We all have problems; what's yours?" She went on to say she had been married 45 years to a darling man and he had just died suddenly. I tried to cheer her. The lifesaver came along. I was glad of that. He took her to the hospital. I often wondered how she was doing. I hoped I gave her something to live for.

I had many calls and visits from Jim and Reg. They both offered me lots of dinners out, etc. that I hadn't accepted yet. I seemed to be living in a different world since Fred died. Maybe I should accept Reg's offer of a vacation somewhere, but where, I just couldn't think. I would talk to Reg when he came around. He would have something planned. He had had this on his mind for some weeks.

Reg and I had just returned to my apartment after a lovely dinner out. As we walked in, the phone was ringing. At first I couldn't understand the accent of the person who was speaking. "Remember me? I am Peter Townley; you saved my life on the beach some weeks ago."

"Oh, Peter, I had forgotten you. How are you?"

"I want to take you out for a nice dinner. When can I see you?" I couldn't answer him as Reg was near by me. I asked him to call later in the evening. I had to tell Reg the full story. Reg wasn't too happy about him phoning me. I tried to tell him he was just thanking me again for what I did for him. Peter did phone later but I didn't answer him.

Reg and I spent four days together. We drove up the coast. It was a beautiful drive. It was a brother and sister trip. That I didn't expect, as I had known Reg a long time now. But I enjoyed the relaxing journey. I realised he was not another Fred to me.

I got another begging letter from Ann. When was I coming back to the USA? I realised what she was trying to tell me. It was quite a begging letter for me to return to my birthplace. I would think about it and write her later.

It was some weeks later when I got that old feeling to return to California. I talked to Reg about it. He wasn't very helpful. He didn't say yes you should or even no, stay here. I could see he wasn't too happy at the idea of me leaving him now. After all, we did have a lot in common. Also, he told me he loved me dearly and hated the idea. I wouldn't talk to him about it again.

We had a big party coming off in the hotel sometime the following week, so I must give all my help. They had been so kind to me I couldn't let them down. I didn't know it was all the real estate owners who were celebrating their big season. I loved these parties. I always had fun and usually met someone nice. I was looking forward to it.

We had a busy time at the hotel preparing for this big affair. It seemed it was a dinner and a dance afterwards. We had a large dance hall that adjoined the hotel. I usually ended up at the dance after the pub had closed.

We had the best night ever. I was so busy I didn't have much time to talk to these people. One gentleman made himself known to me. I couldn't place him for a few minutes. Then it came to me he was in real estate. He was Frank Holden with a Bronx address. He was over here on a visit with some friends who were in real estate. So after dinner he asked me to dance with him. Frank was a well-preserved man in his sixties, I guessed, and was a beautiful dancer. I liked the way he held me. I could nearly feel his heart beat.

The drinks were really flowing. I got to the state where I needed some loving. I had been neglected for some time.

As the dance cam to a close at 2:00 a.m. he introduced me to the friends he was staying with. To me they looked quite prosperous. I accepted an invitation for drinks the day after. Frank picked me up about 2:00 and we had a drive along the coast. He was a very interesting man. He told me he had been divorced three times and was a bachelor now; never had any children, he said to his sorrow. I did console him. I had one son, but I only saw him once a year, maybe. So children can make one happy; they can also make one sad at times.

I was surprised as we drew up to the house where Frank was staying. It was an old English castle type. It really amazed me as Frank pulled a bell and a maid in uniform invited us in. Then the lady of the house came to greet us and we adjourned to a fabulous old English parlour. It took my breath away. As time went on I noticed there was no husband around, only a Mr. Wentworth she introduced me to. Maybe she was divorced. I kind of put two and two together and I came to the conclusion she was also a single lady and Mr. Wentworth was her sleeping partner.

Frank didn't tell me much about her and I didn't ask any questions as she was a wonderful hostess. We had a lovely evening. Frank brought me home but he didn't come in, just a peck on the cheek and a "Good night, darling." He wasn't the pushing sort of fellow; I guess a slow worker.

I hadn't seen Reg for nearly a week now and I hadn't phoned him. He knew I was busy in the hotel. Even so he always called me. Maybe he thought I had decided to return to California. If I did decide to return to California, that would be the end of Reg and me. Our love would fade for each other. I didn't like to think this would happen. I still had a soft spot for Reg.

I think this hotel business spoiled me. I had so many admirers, but I loved it. What more could a woman want with all these admirers? It kept me young and happy.

Frank phoned me and asked if he could see me again, but I felt I didn't want to start another love affair. Reg was enough for me now, so I refused him and said I was busy at the hotel. Also I was moving into a new flat. The hotel got too near for me. I was called on to work too much.

I got settled down in my new home, all new furniture, everything I always had before. I had the same phone number, so I got another call from Frank. "Darling, I must see you. I have a lot to tell you. When can I see you?" This was a shock to me. I thought I'd finished him off by refusing to see him. He wouldn't take no for an answer, so I gave him my new address and he was around to see me within a half hour. I was really stuck for words as to what to say to him. But, he greeted me with a big hug and a kiss on the lips. It really surprised me, but I took it for what it seemed, just a passing flirtation. We drank tea for about an hour. I was very interested in his proposal, not of marriage, but a business he wanted me to go into partnership with right here in England. I was really surprised that he would think of staying here for that one reason as he left England a long time ago and had, I understood, a prosperous real estate business in the Bronx. It seemed these friends had talked him into opening an office here at the coast. Frank suggested I could manage it. I told him I didn't know anything about real estate. He replied, "Don't worry, dear; I'll put you through your exams." Well, this was a shock to me. I told him I would have to think it over. Frank left after two hours of trying to convince me.

I just had to sit down and relax after he left, as I couldn't bring myself to any decision. Maybe I'd talk it over with Reg.

Reg still hadn't called to see me at the hotel. He knew where to find me. The hotel manager could tell him if he was interested enough. I just let the days go by, hoping Reg would phone me. The only phone calls I got were from Frank asking me if I had decided yet. I told him I couldn't give him an answer yet. I much think this offer over more seriously. I felt I wanted someone else's opinion. Every time the phone rang I was hoping to hear Reg's voice. I had waited too long to hear from him so I decided I should be the one to break the quietness between us. I called three times. No answer came. I decided to let him phone me if he needed me. Maybe he was trying to be hard to get. If he was, I was not chasing after him. I had too many admirers to worry about one man, although Reg was always there when I needed him.

Another phone call from Frank, I presumed, so I didn't answer it. Frank was really the type that wouldn't give up. I had to admire him for this. I guess this was why he had a prosperous real estate business in the Bronx, USA. It was too soon for me to make up my mind regards Frank's offer. He would have to give me more time to decide. I may change my mind and return to California. My sister was pressuring me to return to meet this Scot she talked about. I didn't feel very interested just then at meeting him.

I had not told Frank I had ideas of returning to California. I didn't think he would offer this partnership had he known that.

Some weeks had passed and no phone calls or visits to the hotel from Reg. I just couldn't understand why, so I phoned him again and was told the phone was taken off. Well, that really did worry me. Where could Reg be? He had never done this to me. The night I was in the hotel a stranger spoke to me and asked if I knew of a man called Reg. He didn't mention his surname, so I told him I did. "He does come into the hotel now and then, but he hasn't been seen for several weeks." As he talked about Reg he pulled from his pocket an identification badge. I was shocked to see he was a private detective. I asked why he thought I would know where he was. He replied that some of the men who came into this hotel told him I was a dear friend of his. I told this detective I had not seen Reg for nearly six weeks and I didn't know where he was, as I had tried to phone him and the phone was off. I didn't talk too long as I had nothing to tell him. This was a very distressing time for me. I just didn't understand it. Reg wasn't the kind of person who would just be oblivious to any situation.

It was two months now and no word of Reg. This was a mystery to me. I felt Reg wouldn't do anything unkind to hurt me. Frank was still asking me to decide about his new partnership. I wasn't in the mood to make any decisions to Frank. But I thought I would decide to go into real estate with the help of Frank. His could be the answer to my confusion now. I promised Frank I'd call him later.

I was still worried about Reg. This really was a mystery to me. He was such a kind person, I couldn't think what might happen to him. It seemed the detectives were looking for him. He wasn't the type who would hurt anyone.

The days went by and no news of Reg. I had to make up my mind if I wanted to start in real estate or return to California; this would be a very hard decision for me to make.

I got a phone call from the police station asking me if I could come to identify a body. I felt sure it wouldn't be Reg. Within a half hour a policeman picked me up to go to the morgue to identify two bodies. Gosh, two bodies! Why do they want me? I guess with me working in the hotel bars, I would know who they were. I didn't like to do this, but if I could be of any help, I would.

As we arrived, there was quite a confusion amongst the policemen. I couldn't catch what they were saying.

To my shock one of these bodies was Reg. Seems the police picked him up for being drunk and disturbing the peace, and there was a struggle between Reg and the officer. Somehow, Reg was shot accidentally by the policeman. This is what the police told me had happened to Reg. I just could not believe this. Reg never had too many drinks when he was with me, but I did know he drank a lot at times at parties, etc.

This was the result of my working in hotels; one meets some funny characters.

Chapter Fourteen.

Now I could settle down to studying real estate. I was looking forward to having my own business, with the help of Frank.

I made a new circle of friends. This was going to be a new life for me, but I still helped out at the hotel one day a week. I liked to keep in touch with these people. It would also help my business.

The weeks seemed to pass so quickly and I made my first sale. It was a big fabulous house on the sea front. It belonged to a widower; his wife had died suddenly and he decided to go and live in Spain. I had lots of time to talk to him about living in Spain. I told him I had been there for a long weekend, and loved it. It surprised me when he gave me an invitation to visit him in Spain when he got settled down. I accepted his invitation, but months went by and I never heard from him, so I guessed he was just being polite to me.

I was learning more about real estate every day, and I was ready for having my own business. I didn't tell Frank yet, but I was looking around for a suitable place for an office. My life seemed to have settled down more - no love affairs as yet. I got a feeling of neglect at times; no one loved me, and this manly love is what I shall always need. It keeps me young to think I am capable of attracting this kind of love. I have promised myself to love and be loved by all, as God loved the world.

I didn't hear from Spain. His name was Thomas Worthing. I had been referring to him as Mr. Spain to my friends, but to him I must call him Thomas, not Tom. I must not get too eager to hear from him; he had to settle down.

We had four more sales persons working from this office. There was a wife and husband team. I became quite friendly with the wife. She and her hubby were members of a church not far from the office. She asked me to attend one of the services. I did promise her I would one day; just now I was too busy thinking of having my own real estate business.

Frank was very pleased with my big sale. I knew he had suspicions that I intended to start my own business soon. He gave me a hint that he may be returning to America.

Weeks had passed and Frank asked me if I'd be interested in buying out his real estate business. I was not surprised at this. I told him I'd give it a thought.

This must sound strange, but I became a member of this little church not far from our office. I was really enjoying the people. They were open-minded; they knew I worked in a pub.

I bought Frank's business and I kept on his staff. This worked up to a very prosperous business. I had six sales people now.

But somehow this business didn't do anything for me. I was missing the hotel life. I decided to quit. I sold out at a good price. Frank had returned to the USA. I didn't hear from him.

It was a relief for me to be free again without any responsibilities. I was feeling kind of lonesome. I took my care and drove up the coast and parked my car as near the ocean as I could, just to watch the waves roll in. My mind seemed to be in the same state as the ocean, just rolling from one idea to another. What was it I wanted out of life? My life was empty; no one loved me. I couldn't take this any longer.

I drove higher up the coast and noticed a very nice hotel. It attracted me and I went in. They were just serving afternoon tea. I was ready for a cup of tea.

This was a good class hotel. I could see by the clientele. They were busy in the bar. The manager cam to greet me and wished me a beautiful day. I talked for an hour. He informed me this hotel was up for sale. This really hit me like a bombshell. I got some funny ideas; shall I buy it? How much was it? I made more inquiries. It was going to be sold by owner; that sounded good to me.

I had an interview with the owner; he was a Scot, I'd have to keep an eye on him; Scots are keen buyers and salesmen. He gave me a figure that really floored me. I would have to sell my houses to buy it.

I got home, to sit and dream of the hotel. This was just what I wanted. I returned the next day to really look it over. It had two bars, four drinking rooms, six rooms above, four bathrooms - this appealed to me. From the front sitting room I could watch the ocean. It was so peaceful; I felt like this was what I needed.

I got in touch with my solicitor. I sold most of my properties and bought the hotel.

The staff stayed on so there were no problems. I was just loving every minute of it. The manager also was a real Scot; his name was Ian Morrison. He sure knew his job; he managed to keep the staff happy.

I had very little work to do. My job was to mix in with the customers. This I was enjoying. I met a lot of eligible men, young and old, who might solve my problems.

I had not been to church for some weeks now. I made an effort to attend a celebration for the minister and his wife. They had been there for 10 years. There was a party at the church secretary's apartment. I was surprised to see there was champagne and wine and lots of goodies to eat. Jerry, the church secretary, was a very fine, attractive looking man. The first time I met him he told me he had never been married, but was still looking for Mrs. Right.

It was getting towards 11:00 o'clock, so the party came to an end. After a lot of good-nights and hugs we left for home. To my surprise, Jerry offered to drive me home, but I had my own car. As I was ready to drive off he leaned over and gave me a real smacking kiss on the lips. I really was quite shocked. He then asked if he could see me again for a dinner date. I didn't know how to answer him. I suggested he should come up to the hotel. He didn't know I had moved.

After I left him I realised I'd left my house keys on the settee, so I had to go back to Jerry's apartment for them. I didn't like the idea of doing this at midnight, and I knew Jerry lived alone. This I had to do. As I rang the bell there was no answer. I gave it two pushes. I could hear the bell was ringing. I was getting scared but I pushed the bell once more. I could hear some movement inside.

At last Jerry opened the door. He was speechless. He didn't know what was the idea of my return. I tried to tell him; at last he said, "Please come in." I had a very guilty feeling. When I told him I'd left my keys on the sofa, he went for his dressing gown as he was just in his pyjamas. I apologised to him for disturbing him, but he assured me that it was a pleasure to see me again and he suggested he would make me a cup pf tea. I thought that was sweet of him. I accepted his kindness.

We sat on the same settee and talked for an hour, mostly about himself. He said he had been the church's secretary for only six months. He remarked he wasn't really interested in church work and would like a different job. I told him I may be able to fix him into my hotel job. He was really delighted with the idea. I said I would talk to him later about this, so it was just a handshake and a 'good night Pat', not even a kiss on the cheek.

On my way home I was driving kind of slow. That was a good thing to do at 1:00 a.m. I suddenly noticed something in the road. I couldn't see too well as it was a dark night. I switched my big beams on, and behold, it was a body. I pulled up to the side of the road, and went to see what or who it was. I got a kind of scared feeling. When I looked again I could see it was a man. He looked so young, maybe in his forties. So I dragged his body to the curb side. He sure seemed to me dead. I tried to move his arms up and down; I thought it may help him.

All at once he moved. Gee, I was really getting more scared than ever. What shall I do? I started to talk to him, but he just stared at me.

I got in my car and went to the nearest phone booth. I managed to get the police, and the ambulance came. The police asked me all kinds of funny questions I didn't like. They thought I had run over him. Now I was beginning to be sorry I even stopped. I'd got myself into something I'd have to prove I didn't do.

It was 2:00 a.m. when I arrived home. I couldn't sleep for thinking what will be the outcome of this kindness I did for this person.

I didn't hear anything from the police for months, so I didn't call them. I thought I'd leave well alone.

I told my manager Ian. I called him John, as Ian is Scotch for John. He said I was very brave to have stopped at that time of night. He told me I had a visitor, a gentleman. John described him as quite a gentleman in his fifties. John was always interested in a person's appearances. "Didn't you ask him his name?" Yes, he did, but had forgotten it. He said he would be in the hotel the day after. I just couldn't think who this interesting gentleman could be. It could be Mr. Spain, Thomas Worthing. I was hoping it was.

Yes, it was Mr. Spain; as John said he looked a prosperous gentleman. He gave me quite a thrill. There are not many men like him around these days. We both seemed happy to meet again after a lapse of time; it must be six months.

Thomas said he was settled down in his new home and was ready for me to visit him. He suggested I should fly back with him when he left. That kind of excited me. I gave him a look of acceptance. In return he said, "Let's make a date." I was ready any time, but Thomas said he had some business to attend to before he left. "Let's say in two weeks, Pat." That suited me fine. I was feeling I needed this break away from the hotel. I didn't have any worries regarding John's management; he was the tops.

Thomas was in the hotel most days. He took me out for dinner several days. I got to know him better.

Off we went to Spain. As we landed at the airport, Thomas picked up a very nice car and we drove along the coast for about 15 miles. It was a beautiful day, not too warm. Thomas was not too talkative as we drove to his home. He seemed to have other things on his mind besides me.

My mind was wandering a little too. What kind of house has he? I do know property is cheaper in Spain. I may be interested in buying there, who knows?

At last we arrived at his home. I could see this house was newly built and quite spacious. It had a commanding appearance like a castle type. The entrance hall was huge. I noticed everywhere I looked was immaculate. It hardly looked lived in.

There didn't seem to be anyone living there. Just then a couple of dogs came to greet us. They were very friendly and believe it or not one was called Pat. I thought Thomas was talking to me.

Suddenly there appeared a grey-haired lady in her sixties. Thomas introduced me to her as his housekeeper. She was French but spoke good English. She greeted me very warmly. I liked her from our first meeting. We became very close friends. She told me some very precious secrets about Thomas' past. I was very surprised, but one never knows. You can't judge a sausage by its skin. I had to call her Liz. Maybe one day I'd need her help.

The first day there was wonderful. I seemed to be living in another world. I have lived in so many different worlds, but this seemed different from them all. It was a different atmosphere, something I couldn't place. The days went by too quickly. Thomas had been a perfect gentleman in a way I couldn't understand. There was no love making, not even a good night kiss. What is this man thinking of? Maybe I am not his cup of tea, as they say in England. I tried to work out what could be missing in my make-up. I am a very lovable person; I felt surely he recognised this. I did give him a hug and a peck on his cheek, but that didn't bring anything out of him. He seemed really bottled up with his feelings. This surely did puzzle me.

We spend six beautiful days driving, and lounging around the pool. The day before I left, we seemed to have a better understanding of each other. He became more at ease with me. He told me he had a brother who was a builder that lived just up the coast from him, was once married to a French gal but was divorced and had an English gal living with him. I told Thomas I'd love to meet this English gal. Also his brother. Thomas remarked, "Next time you come, Pat, I will let you meet them." I thought, is there going to be a next time? I hope so; it sounds interesting.

I still wasn't satisfied with Thomas' behaviour towards me. I had never met a man who had got me guessing. I couldn't solve his attitude towards life. There was something missing somewhere, although he was kind to me. There must be a method in his madness.

I noticed when he gave me a tour of his house he missed opening one room for me to see. I remember it was next to the bathroom. I was tempted to try to open it, but it was locked. That made me very suspicious. What could be in there? Maybe my visit will be more explanatory. My thought world really went wild. Could he be a con man, a drug dealer or what?

I hoped I was not judging him wrongly. Thomas had been so generous to me. He took me to the airport. As we said goodbye, I thanked him once again for his hospitality. He held my hand in a manner like he didn't want to let go of it. "Pat, please come again soon. I shall miss you." With a big hug and a brotherly kiss he said, "Take care of yourself, Pat. Just remember there aren't many like us left in this world." I wondered what he meant by that.

I felt kind of sad leaving him. He had some fine qualities I had not recognised yet. I realised Thomas wasn't going to fall in love with love; he was waiting for the person who could replace his wife of 20 years.

When I arrived home John had lots of news for me. He said there was a visit from the police, making inquiries about the fellow I had found lying in the road some weeks ago. The police wanted to know how I had found him, or had I knocked him down? They came to see I was pleased to tell them the truth. Now the police told me this fellow, named Bill Pollard, wanted to meet me to personally thank me for what I did to help him. Seems he had been to a party and was crossing the road and slipped and hit his head. That knocked him out. No one had run him down. This was the police report.

I was pleased to meet this Bill Pollard. He seemed a very likeable fellow in his fifties. He told me quite a lot of his personal life - the usual, was married and now divorced, living alone and no children. What a blessing, I thought.

He made a habit of visiting the hotel, and he always asked for me. I got to know this Bill. He was a very plausible sort of fellow, but I needed to know him a bit longer. I must not encourage him.

John also said some fellow called and gave his name as just Jerry. This was expected from Jerry. He called again and I was there to answer him. He made lots of excuses as to why he had not called before. He told me he'd left the church secretary's job and he was managing a hotel in Brighton, about 10 miles from here. It was nearer to London. I promised I would call to see him one day. He told me quite a lot about this hotel; it interested me.

I did keep my promise and went to see Jerry. This was a larger hotel than mine. They catered and had a swimming pool. It was a beautiful hotel. It was residential, too; they had many people staying there.

I really enjoyed the visit and I started to make a habit of seeing Jerry at least once a week. This hotel was doing something for my ego. Also, I was meeting a different kind of people. I found myself visiting this hotel many times in a week. I joined a mah-jong club. That game always fascinated me. I became very popular and had many invitations out for dinner. These men were mostly retired, in their early sixties, well preserved. Some looked like they had never done a day's work in their lives.

One of these men was very persistent, begging me for a date for dinner with him. They called him Peter. He seemed to be a favourable person around them. I had to admit he was attractive. I had heard all kinds of rumours about this Peter. I just couldn't believe all I heard, although I was hoping it was true. He was a man who a woman would be proud to own, but he had been married twice.

I seemed to have lost interest in my own hotel. I was too busy visiting Jerry's hotel. It was named the Sea Shore Hotel. I didn't rename my hotel; it was always known as the Beach Hotel.

I liked Brighton. They had a bigger population and they got more visitors, which made the hotel business prosperous.

Peter knew I owned a hotel and said he would like to visit me. I gave him a very pressing invitation, "Please do, Peter. Let me know when you intend to come and I'll make sure I'll be there."

I enjoyed his company and he took me out for dinner after several visits. He said he liked my hotel and thought it had possibilities of enlarging it, similar to the Sea Shore Hotel. This gave me a thought; maybe I would do that, with the help of Peter.

Peter became a very dear friend to me, not a lover as yet, just a good friend. But, to me he was more than a good friend. My feelings for him were growing stronger. This I must control. Peter hadn't shown any love for me yet, but his kindness to me had a reason.

Jerry had noticed that Pete was showing a great interest in me. Jerry told me some very surprising things about Peter. It was hard for me to believe him. Peter had a very young blonde housekeeper and they all presumed he was living with her. I didn't believe this because he was free to visit me any time. I don't think if she was his lover she would allow him out of her sight - this was the least of my worries about Peter.

Also, Jerry confidentially told me Peter was the biggest share-holder in the Sea Shore Hotel. He practically owned the hotel. Well, I guess there will always be rumours. I would wait until Peter was ready to tell me about this young blonde housekeeper.

I had a phone call from Thomas. He informed me he and his brother would be over here soon, so I invited them to stay at my hotel. I wondered what the idea was of bringing his brother. I had never met him.

I found Thomas' brother a very interesting person. He was another William. No, we had to call him William, not Bill. He liked the hotel but the thought it could be enlarged to look more prosperous. The more I thought of their suggestions, the more I felt I should do something. I asked William to give me an idea of what I should do to the hotel, maybe more rooms and a pool. This was just a thought for me.

I still liked the idea of living in Spain. California seemed too far away. But I still had my house there, should I decide to live there. Just now I was enjoying life. Thomas and Peter had fulfilled my happiness. Why should I change it?

William was a very likeable fellow. His advice about my hotel I didn't accept. I had a feeling I wouldn't be living there much longer, maybe in Spain or elsewhere. William gave me an invitation to see his house. This I promised him.

I got a phone call from Ann. She wanted to come over for a visit with me. She sounded kind of fed up with life in general. I asked her how her love life was. She answered me in a way I would think she was weeping. I begged her to tell me what the problem was. But she said she would tell me all when she arrived here, in two weeks.

I told her about Peter. Also that I had been to Spain. It cheered her up a little. I told her I would take her to Spain to meet William. I knew she would be interested in meeting him. Ann didn't mention the Scotch fellow. Maybe he had remarried.

I seemed to have a lot of visitors now. My son and his new wife arrived unexpectedly. Seems he had an appointment for a new job in London. I was pleased about that. I hoped they would come to live here.

This was my first meeting of David's new wife. She seemed much younger than he. I was surprised to hear both his children were married. He never let me know when. I never heard from them only at Christmas to thank me for the checks I sent them.

I took David and his wife to meet Peter. They were very impressed with this Sea Shore Hotel. Peter invited them to stay there for a few days. This did surprise me. David told me a few interesting affairs that Peter had encountered in his life.

Peter had been mixed up in a big gambling deal and he had lost a lot of money. He also told David he had been married twice, but was hoping to remarry again, some day when he found the right lady. He also remarked how he was very fond of me. That was something I didn't expect from Peter, as he had never shown any love for me as yet. I guessed he would be a hard-to-get person. I didn't want to seem to be over-anxious.

Thomas was a fine man whom I was interested in. As regards marriage, I could not decide on anyone. They both were very suitable men to marry.

Peter was kind enough to take me to the airport to meet Ann. I was really surprised to see Ann had lost some weight. It made her look much younger. As I introduced her to Peter she seemed to glow with expectations, and I noticed peter really looked her over and made a big fuss of her. Well, if Peter could make her happy with her stay here, that would suit me.

Ann had been with me two days and that phone had not stopped ringing. It was Peter phoning Ann asking her to come and see him. At last he came to pick up Ann and take her out for dinner. I felt kind of hurt; he didn't ask me to go along with them. So now it's all Ann with Peter. I'll just leave them to it.

I was amazed when Ann told me she was going to stay for a few days with Peter. This was a shock to me. He didn't work so fast when I first met him. Maybe it was love at first sight. I hoped he wasn't playing funny tricks with Ann, but she was old enough to look after herself. Ann had not told me about her love life in America. I guess she would when she had the opportunity. Right now she was playing a funny game with Peter.

I didn't think Ann would consider living in England again. I kept my word and I took Ann to Spain to meet Thomas and his brother William. We stayed at Thomas' house for three days. Then William invited us to see his house. I had told Ann about William's blonde housekeeper, but when we arrived he had an elderly grey-haired lady he introduced as his housekeeper. Where was the blonde? As we were given a tour of his beautiful house, he remarked that this bedroom was his niece's room, but she had left to be with her sick mother. So I guess that is the answer to a tall story. After all, William was not living with a young blonde. I was happy about that.

William was very happy to meet Ann. There seemed to be an attraction between them. We four went out together driving and swimming. Thomas was by my side most of the time. Ann and William left us to take a jaunt up the coast. We were happy to lounge near the pool. Thomas asked me if I had thought about Spain again, and "do you think you will build a house there?"

I told him I had an interest in a Brighton hotel, so he didn't press for the answer.

We had stayed at William's house for nearly a week. I told Ann we were wearing out our welcome; we had better leave soon. Ann didn't like that idea. Also, William said to me there was no hurry for Ann and me to leave just yet.

Thomas would visit us most every day, but we decided I should leave Ann at William's home and I would stay with Thomas. They were pleased with the idea, so Thomas and I left the two lovebirds, and we enjoyed being alone.

Four days passed and not a phone call from Ann, so I phoned them to ask, "When do we leave for England?" The reply wasn't too enthusiastic. I told Ann it was a must that I return at once to my home as I had a lot of commitments to attend to. She eventually agreed we should leave for home. The men took us to the airport. Ann and William were sad at parting. He kept repeating to Ann, "Please come back soon."

Well, I was glad to get home again. Ann didn't say much about William, only that he was paying her a lot of attention, but she didn't think he was serious.

One week had passed and who dropped in the hotel but William. Well, Ann was thrilled to bits. He didn't stay with us. I recommended the Sea Shore at Brighton and that's where he stayed, but he was up here every day. Ann didn't go to see Peter again. She was afraid it would make William jealous.

William was here for two weeks. I thought he would never leave. Ann seemed so happy I had to ask her, "Are you serious with William?"

She looked at me with a gleam in her eyes and said "Look what William bought me."

That was a shocker to me. It was a beautiful diamond ring. I was speechless. "Ann," I said, "what does this mean? Are you engaged to be married to William?"

She was slow at answering me. "Darling, I'm not sure yet. I have to give him my answer before he leaves tomorrow."

This was too, too quick an affair for it to last, I thought. I asked Ann so many questions. "Are you going to live in Spain or what have you decided to do?" No, she hadn't decided on anything yet.

William left and I just couldn't bring myself to ask Ann what she had decided to do regards William. He phoned her every day. Ann was due to leave for California in three days.

The day before she left she confessed to me about William. He wanted to marry her as soon as she said yes. But Ann told me she didn't want to marry anyone. She just wanted William as her lover. I was very upset about this. I wished she would marry and settle down with someone. I thought William would make a good husband. I couldn't understand Ann not wanting to marry William. There was something that was preventing her from marrying. Ann left me with an open mid. I thought she was attached to some fellow in California. I knew when she arrived here she was in a state of confusion. She didn't tell me her problems. In a way I was pleased she had returned to California. Now I could settle down to my own problems.

Thomas phoned me several times. He didn't mention Ann. He asked me if he could visit me again soon. I didn't refuse him, but we didn't make a date. I thought I'd just leave it for him to decide when he should visit me. Our conversation wasn't too happy. I had a strong feeling something was worrying him. Maybe he was concerned about his brother's love affair with Ann.

As usual I went to the Sea Shore Hotel to play mah-jong. I saw peter but there was a strange feeling between us. He didn't inquire about Ann, and I was not interested in their affairs. I think Ann got the wrong impression from Peter. He wasn't the type of fellow who fell for these women who were looking for a husband. With his experiences, he knew women.

Just a week went by and Thomas phoned to say he would arrive the day after. I was pleased he was coming; maybe we could get a better understanding. I would insist he stay with me.

Thomas hired a car so I didn't meet him at the airport. I got quite a thrill to see him again. He was the finest person I had met in a long time. I always felt happy and content to be with him. Yet he wasn't my lover. He had not tried to prove his manhood to me yet. We both had a mutual feeling with each other. Although my sex life had been sadly neglected, I didn't seem to be in a great hurry to expect Thomas to prove anything to me. I liked him the way he was. As we grew together to love each other, our sex life would become more sacred.

Thomas stayed with me for two weeks and no mention of him returning to Spain. We seemed to have lots of things to talk about. He did tell me he had been married twice. His first wife died in a strange accident. He didn't say what happened, and I didn't press him to tell me. His second wife divorced him, on what grounds I really had no idea. He was such a kind person, but I guess one has to live with a person to really know him.

Ann had been home three weeks now and she had not phoned me. She had me guessing as to what her plans were. Was she going to marry William and live in Spain, or maybe William would like to live in California. I wished she would phone me.

Thomas had never mentioned Ann and William. Maybe he didn't know much, and I was not going to inquire. Ann would have to tell me when she was ready. Thomas wanted me to return to Spain with him, but I told him I had a lot of things to do and lots on my mind.

I was seriously thinking of selling my hotel. I had lost interest in it since I met Thomas. I just may buy a house in Spain. I still had a rented house here. If I changed my mind I could always live here in Hastings.

I didn't tell Thomas what was on my mind. I was waiting for him to make the first move. If he asked me to marry him, I felt sure I would accept his offer of marriage. I had got to the stage I wanted to settle down to a quiet life, maybe in Spain or California.

I wished Ann would phone me. If I only knew what she had decided to do, I could make up my mind to do something.

Thomas went home with just a big hug and kiss on the cheek, and he reminded me that he loved me very dearly and would I consider him as my future husband? I thought that was a strange proposal of marriage. I just gave him an assuring smile and waved him goodbye. I didn't go to the airport to see him off. Maybe he did expect me to take him to the airport. I seemed to have a lot on my mind and I didn't think of it.

Thomas never failed to phone me every day. He gave me a little news about William. He was selling his house. Well, that was a surprise. I told Thomas I might be interested in buying it. I was very impressed with William's house. It was much bigger than Thomas' house and had a bigger pool and deck. Thomas suggested I should come over and have another look at it. I told him I wanted to hear from Ann, just to hear what she had on her mind.

It was six weeks since Ann left. I decided to phone her. She told me William was selling his house in Spain and was going to live in California. No mention of her marrying William. I really got cross with her. "Ann, you must tell me your intentions with William. Are you going to marry him now, or later?" She was slow to answer me. I repeated my question to her. "Ann, please tell me, do you intend to marry William?"

"Darling, I can't say right now. William is going to buy a house near me, and he is hoping I'll marry him soon. But, Pat, I just can't make up my mind. I am very fond of William, but as to marriage, I am not ready to marry anyone at present."

"But, Ann, why do you encourage William to live in California? I wish you would be honest with him. William is a very nice fellow. Please don't fool him."

I decided to put my hotel up for sale. It took just three weeks to sell it, so I moved into my house in Hastings. I had it rented and furnished, so there was no problem. I had not many things to move from the hotel.

I felt kind of relieved to be in my own house again. Thomas was shocked to hear this news, and he came over to see what I had decided to do regarding William's house. I seemed to be going round in circles. Ann had really upset my plans for my future.

Thomas was a godsend for me right now. He took me out for dinner every day he was here. I told him about Ann. She couldn't make up her mind if she wanted to marry William. Thomas told me William was crazy about Ann and wanted to marry her now.

I went back to Spain with Thomas. We went to see William's house. I really fell in love with it. William was very keen on selling his house. I didn't ask any questions as to why he was selling, only that he had decided to live in California. He didn't mention Ann. I thought that was very confusing to me. Ann was my sister; he must realise I was interested in her welfare.

We returned to Thomas' house. After dinner we got down to a serious talk. Thomas was very concerned about William and did not like the idea of him living in California. I told him William must know what he wanted out of life; it might change his outlook on his future living.

Thomas was slow at talking about our future. I didn't know how I could start to talk about us. I asked him if he thought it wise for me to buy William's house; it was kind of big for one person. Yes, he agreed with me. "But Pat, dear, you are used to a big place to live. After living in a hotel you might feel you are limited to space in a smaller house." We didn't talk about us. I got the feeling he was more concerned about his brother than about our future.

I couldn't decide if I should buy William's house, so I thought it best I should return home and try to relax. Thomas did not want me to leave so soon. I'd only been there three days. He suggested we should take a drive up the coast somewhere. We spent three more days together. Thomas was still a gentleman to me. He had a funny way of showing his love for me, not a sexual love, but truly affectionate love. He was of the old fashioned type of persons who believe in waiting until one is married before having sex. I had never met a man like Thomas with those kinds of ideals. I guess I must have patience with Thomas. He must have something else on his mind that was preventing him from asking me to be his wife.

I returned home with a very unsettled feeling. Do I buy William's house or do I not? Does Thomas want to marry me or does he not? I wish I knew.

I got a phone call from Ann. To my surprise she told me she was going to marry William. That sure was a surprise for me. The last time I had heard from her she wasn't ready to marry anyone. I asked her what made her change her mind. Seems she had been having a strong love affair on a promise of marriage, and he just said goodbye and that was the last she heard of him. He lived in Canada. Ann had taken this as her last hope of every marrying anyone. Now William must have convinced her of his true love and he wanted to marry her soon.

I asked her was the date made yet for her marriage to William. "Oh, yes, William and I are being married in Las Vegas within two weeks." She wanted Thomas and me to witness it. This was something I would have to consult Thomas about.

I phoned Thomas, but there was no reply. Just three hours after that Thomas was at my door. Well, these people are working fast. "Thomas, what is this unexpected visit? I tried to phone you several times today and got no reply."

"My dear, I was on my way to see you. I have something very exciting to ask you. Pat, darling, will you marry me in Las Vegas? Let's have a double wedding!"

I was speechless for a minute, but I said, "Why Las Vegas? Let's get married here. Then we can go to Las Vegas for our honeymoon."

No, Thomas wanted it to be a double wedding at Las Vegas, so I accepted his offer of marriage. Thomas was so thrilled I had accepted his proposal of marriage. To me, it was different. I had been waiting for this for months.

This marriage to Thomas seemed more like a business transaction. I did realise we were older people, but there was no crazy love-making as yet. I felt there was something missing between us.

I did love Thomas. I hoped I was doing the right thing by marrying him. I would do my best to make it work. I didn't know why my thought world seemed to be spinning around.

Thomas wanted us to live in his house in Spain. That was fine with me. I had my house here so we could share it.

We arrived at Ann's house just a week after Ann had phoned to tell us she was marrying William. We gave her a bigger surprise when Thomas told her we were going to be married and hoped we would have a double wedding in Las Vegas. Ann was really excited at the thought of a double wedding, two brothers marrying two sisters.

We enjoyed the lovely weather in California. Thomas liked it so much he said he would like to live there permanently and sell his house in Spain.

Chapter Fifteen.

Just a few days before we left for Las Vegas, we had a visit from this Scotty fellow whom Ann had told me so much about and wanted me to meet. I was really impressed by his attitude towards me. In front of everyone he gave me a big hug and a kiss. I really felt embarrassed, but I kind of got a thrill from his hug.

When Ann introduced us to him, she gave his name as Allan Gamble. Allan made many excuses to call on Ann. I thought this was too much for me to take. I seemed to have grown an affection for this Scot.

Three days before we were due to leave for Las Vegas, Thomas got a terrible cold and fever. He became very sick and we had to take him to the hospital. The doctors told us he had pneumonia and also a slight stroke; he would be in the hospital for at least a week. This really upset our plans. Allan was very helpful; he took me to the hospital every day.

I was surprised that Ann and William went off to Las Vegas to get married. William was so keen on marrying Ann he couldn't wait until Thomas was better.

Allan took me out for dinner many times. He seemed to be growing closer to me. We both got the same attraction for each other.

Thomas was in the hospital for two weeks. This affection for Allan had grown into true love for each other. We didn't know how to handle this situation. How could we tell Thomas our wedding was off? This feeling of marrying Thomas was not of true love for each other. I always thought Thomas just wanted a housekeeper. He had never shown any true love for me. This Scot had given me more love and understanding within a short time of meeting him. I just couldn't marry Thomas.

We had been at Ann's house now for three weeks. Ann and William were still in Vegas.

I got a phone call from the hospital doctor to advise me Thomas should return home immediately and go into a hospital near his home. This we had to do with the help of Allan. We got Thomas home and into a hospital just a few miles from his home. Allan stayed in a small hotel just up the coast. He came every day to take me to the hospital.

Thomas wasn't doing very well. The doctors told me he would be an invalid for the rest of his life, if he did live after six months. This was a shock to me. Where do I go from here? I just couldn't leave Thomas when he was so sick and probably would not live much longer.

Thomas was able to return home, but needed a lot of help. He could not walk. I stayed with him and got a man to help me. Allan returned to California. We had a phone call from Ann to say there were coming to see Thomas. They would be surprised to see how Thomas had changed from a healthy, strong man to an invalid within such a short time. I now realised that Thomas was not as healthy as he looked. I didn't know he had very high blood pressure, which caused him to have a stroke. The doctor warned me he could have another stroke pretty soon.

Allan phoned me every other day. He was really a sweetheart to me. My love for him seemed to grow more every time he phoned me. When he said goodbye he always told me he loved me. Well, he was a Scot and surely they are very determined people. They always get what they want, in time.

Thomas and William had lots to talk about. Ann was helpful for me. I was glad she was here.

Thomas would often ask me, "Pat, darling, when are we going to get married?"

I had to say, "Just when you say, Thomas."

I found out what Thomas and William were talking about. They had arranged for a minister to come to the house to marry Thomas and me. This was a shock to me. Ann and William witnessed the marriage. What else could I do but say "I do." Thomas seemed to be getting stronger now that we were married.

Allan would phone, but I didn't tell him I had married Thomas. I felt I didn't want to lose his love for me.

Thomas had two more strokes and he died just three months after our marriage. I was glad I married him, because I had promised him I would.

I phoned Allan to tell him the sad news. He said he would be over to see me soon, but I suggested he should wait a few weeks before we could see each other again. I thought it was wise, even in respect to Thomas, that he should not visit me. I think I must have offended Allan. I hadn't heard from him long after Thomas died.

William and Ann came and stayed with me for nearly six weeks. They were a great help to me in my sad loss of Thomas.

I still was feeling my life had taken a turn for the better. I knew I must think this way. One has to respect the dead, but go on and try to live a happy life. I knew it would take some time to realise what had happened to me in such a short time. Being married to Thomas was a very unfulfilled love match. I didn't seem to know him or even love him as I should. He needed me more than I needed him.

When William and Ann left for California, I really felt lonely and I decided to return to England to live. I got a part time job in a very nice hotel not far from Brighton. I met some of the fellows who used to visit my hotel. They were surprised to see me again. They had heard I was married and living in Spain.

I was very surprised that Peter should come to see me. I guess the boys told him where I was. I didn't encourage him as he really was not over-nice to me. He went for Ann in a big way, but Ann didn't accept his love-making as William had arrived on the scene.

I was glad I hadn't sold my home in England. I was enjoying my old friends, and the hotel life seemed to help me forget the things I didn't want to remember. I had so many unhappy memories with my marriages.

It took two weeks before I got my phone in and a new number, so neither Ann nor Allan could phone me.

I had to call Ann. She was surprised I had left Spain and had gone back to live in England. She begged me to return to California to live. I told her I had so many happy memories there that I might think about it one day, but for now I wanted to stay put and relax and wait to see what happened in my love life. I was feeling very cautious as to whom I would marry. Maybe I would never marry again.

I'd been working in this lovely hotel for six weeks and I had made a lot of new friends, most of these men were retired, in their sixties, all married but one - Carl. He had been a widower for two years. He lived alone and had a housekeeper. He had asked me out for dinner several times. I did promise him we would have a day out together. I was not in any mood for dates with anyone at this time.

Carl was very kind to me. He always walked or drove me home after work. I hadn't asked him in for a cup of tea yet. I didn't want to start this until I knew him better. He was a well-known man about town. Everyone seemed to respect him. He was not a woman chaser.

Carl did tell me about his wife. She had suffered from cancer for many years. In the end she took her own life. This must have been a terrible shock for Carl. It could take years for him to recuperate. This seemed to be a very trying time for both of us.

My life seemed very empty now. I had no plans for my future - no real lover to pamper me. I had never felt this way in my whole life. I guess there comes a time in one's life when you have to come to know your real inner self, to know who you are, and cut out your self-pity. This seemed to be my problem. I had been a spoilt person.

I had been taking more walks along the sea front. These waves come in and go out, just like my memories. I sat and watched them. It gave me a feeling of thankfulness. I had lived 57 years. This I had to be thankful for. The more I walked, the more I felt a better person. I met and talked to many people who told me their troubles. It made my problems look small.

It became a habit with me to walk every day for about three miles along the sea front. I would throw a pebble into the sea for a stray dog to retrieve. Dogs can be wonderful friends. They seemed to look forward to seeing me. I sometimes had four or five dogs following me along this sandy beach. There were some rocks I used to sit on and rest. One morning I heard a funny noise which made me get up and look behind the rock I was sitting on. To my surprise there was the body of a man. I thought he was dead, but he moved his head and spoke to me. I asked him if he needed help, but he refused any help.

He got up and sat next to me. His voice sounded very educated. He was a man I would guess in his sixties. I didn't press him to tell me why he was sleeping there. Only, he did say he lived alone and was a lonely person. I could understand now how people could be lonely.

I got up to continue my walk and he asked me if he could walk with me. This I couldn't refuse him. We walked for a few miles; we talked about life and its problems. But, he didn't refer to any outstanding events in his life. He said he had been divorced many years ago and he had no family. To me he looked like he had many problems in the mast. His hair was white; his clothes were clean but unpressed.

I was ready to turn back for home, but he seemed to want to talk more about his past life. So I sat another half hour with him. I thought the poor fellow needed me to listen to him. He kept apologising for what he was about to tell me. I assured him I would listen with an open mind.

He didn't ask my name, but he said, "Can I call you Miss rock? That's where I met you. My name is Peter. They used to call me Pete." I didn't ask him his full name. I just had to call him Pete.

He said he had been married to one woman for 10 years and she fell in love with another man. "I tried to win her back to be but I failed. She wanted a divorce. I had to leave my house and live alone. I was so desperate, I would visit her and beg of her to come back to me. On one of my visits I caught her in bed with her lover. There was a real fight between me and her lover. He took out a gun and was going to shoot me. I was able to get the gun from him and I accidentally shot my wife. She died and I was up for murder."

Pete kept saying, "Please believe me, I didn't do it intentionally." I tried to convince him I believed him. It was hard to judge him.

All this I was trying to piece together. I seemed to follow his story. Then it hit me like a flash! No, no, it couldn't be Pete! Yes, Peter Blair, who had rented one of my apartments 10 years ago. I kept silent for a few minutes. I just couldn't speak. I didn't know what to say to this poor man. I asked him is full name. Yes, he was the same Pete Blair, who rented one of my apartments. I was glad he didn't recognise me.

I made an excuse that I had an appointment soon and I said goodbye and God bless you. He gave me a big smile and a handshake and thanked me for listening. This was a sad meeting for me. As Pete was very kind to me I felt I must return his kindness one day. I hoped I would meet him again and admit to him who I was. I was sure he didn't recognise me. I was glad in a way he didn't know me.

I remember Pete was a solicitor and had a prosperous business until his wife divorced him. Six weeks had passed.

I still had my walks along the beach, but I didn't see Pete. I would like to know what happened to him.

Carl was still around but we didn't seem to make any arrangements for a day out together, as I had promised him I would. He would take me home, but I had not asked him in yet. I didn't know why I felt this way about Carl. Maybe it was because he was a slow worker or he was afraid of women. He also knew I was in no hurry to marry anyone, so we were just good friends.

It would soon be Christmas. I knew the hotel would be very busy with many visitors. I would enjoy the happiness Christmas brings.

I had a phone call from Ann. She and William were going to spend Christmas with me. I was so happy about this. Christmas always brings back sad memories of my marriages. Maybe I would have Carl to join us for Christmas dinner.

Just the week before Christmas, Ann phoned to say they would be with me in two days. I didn't meet them at the airport. I was too busy preparing for their arrival. I was always happy to see William. He was much like my Thomas in looks and his ways. They arrived at my house around 7:00 o'clock. It was then nearly dark. I could only see the car lights and someone getting out of the car. As I opened the door to greet them, there were three people standing there. I couldn't believe my eyes. They had brought Allan the Scotch fellow. Allan gave me a wonderful greeting with a huge bunch of flowers and a big hug. This was my happiest hour. Allan was a great help to me when Thomas died. I can't forget his kindness. I was sorry I had refused to let him come back to Spain to be with me after Thomas had passed away. Maybe that's why he didn't write or contact me until now. I had to apologise to him for my behaviour.

Christmas was here. We had dined and danced. Allan made me hang my stocking up on the bed rail, and it was full of beautiful things, mostly lingerie and night-wear. Yes, a sheer shimmering night gown - I guess his hopes were to see me in it.

We decided we all would spend New Year's Eve in my house in Spain. The weather was beautiful and warm. Allan and I were growing closer as the days went by. They had been here nearly weeks, and no mention of going home yet. Only Ann suggested they were wearing out their welcome and suggested they should leave soon. Allan didn't agree to that. He intended to stay as long as I wanted him.

Ann and William left for California. Allan and I stayed in Spain enjoying the warm weather.

I felt so happy again. Allan had brought more love and understanding into my life than anyone else I had known. I thought he would be the answer to my prayers. He hadn't asked me to marry him yet; there were so many things we had to consider - did I want to leave England and live in California? Sometimes I did; then England just pulled me back to live there.

Spain was all right for a few weeks, but I wouldn't like to live there permanently. So I thought I should take Allan's advice.

We had to return to my home in England. I gave up my job at the hotel. I was enjoying my freedom again and Allan's company.

Allan wasn't rushing me into marrying him; he was only my lover.
I did realise he was a Scot and a very determined person. What he said
he meant and expected me to be honest with him.

I could go on living with him forever. I realised he was the
boss; this I loved. This man knew what he wanted in a woman and I
was going to make him the happiest man alive.

We were married at a small Church of England church not far
from my house. We had dinner at a very nice hotel in Brighton.

There was no question as to where we would live. Yes,
California, here we come. We kept my two houses for holidays in
England and in Spain. We stayed with Ann and William until we
moved into our own house.

This is going to be forever and ever for me. I am a changed
person, not a spoilt person. I feel I have had a very extraordinary life. I
am now ready for a quiet life with Allan.

California is growing on me. This weather is great. I hope to
spend the rest of my life here with Allan. I thank God for his guidance.

Yes, life plays some funny tricks. We have to remember we are
the cause of most of our disappointments in life.

Thank you for reading my book. I think you should know I
have had only two men in my life; one was an alcoholic, the second
was or is a Scot. We have had 25 years of true happiness. We both are
84 years young.

God Bless You.

This was hand written by my mother around 1960. The hotels
where she served her 'apprenticeship' were, first, The Hargreaves
Arms in Accrington, where her father was the licensee. Mother and
sister Alice worked the bar, where she met my father. An older sister
married and moved to America, the next oldest was in charge of the
kitchen. The oldest brother died in the First World War, the second
also married and went to America.

A room was used for using a cinematograph, admission being
one penny or two jam jars. The man who owned the equipment later
opened the first cinema in Accrington. He offered a partnership to her
father, but was turned down, after all, it was just a passing fancy! A
larger rear room was the Masonic Temple.

They then moved to The Ogden Arms in Manchester - now known as The Rembrandt. After only a few months her father succumbed to pernicious anaemia, so easy to cure these days. Her mother managing on a widows pension till 1948, when I was doing National Service in Egypt.

She was an excellent dressmaker, and in later years supplemented the family income regularly, by making dresses and loose covers. Her Second World War experiences were as written - including the Alnwick Castle Ball, and driving a Joe Lyons tea van.

I narrowly missed being sent to Canada on the City of Benares - sunk by U Boat with great loss of life.

The rest of the story is as she would have liked it to be. Coming back to reality at the very end. The Newcastle flat was sold, sharing the proceeds with my father. He quite happily gambled and drank his half, but mother bought a ticket on the Queen Mary. She was met in New York by a widowed brother-in-law, a retired ships Chief Engineer, Allan Houston. She later described this as akin to being struck by lightning. The Greyhound bus ticket was returned, a car hired for a trip through the Rockies, to Reno. Divorced and married there, they eventually bought a bungalow in San Clemente, living happily in California, sharing thirty years.

This was typed in America, and spent many years in her garage, before it came to me. Editing has been difficult, mainly involving typos. I wanted to keep the 'voice' of the early 1900's intact. I hope I've managed that.

I also hope you have enjoyed this voyage through my mother's imagination.

David Mason. (Not divorced!)

Lightning Source UK Ltd.
Milton Keynes UK
03 February 2011
166890UK00001B/68/P